THE NATION OF ISLAM,
AN AMERICAN MILLENARIAN MOVEMENT

THE NATION OF ISLAM,
AN AMERICAN MILLENARIAN MOVEMENT

Martha F. Lee

Studies in Religion and Society
Volume 21

The Edwin Mellen Press
Lewiston/Queenston
Lampeter

Library of Congress Cataloging-in-Publication Data

Lee, Martha F. (Martha Frances), 1962-
  The Nation of Islam, an American Millenarian Movement / Martha F.
Lee.
    p. cm. -- (Studies in religion and society ; v. 21)
  Bibliography: p.
  Includes index.
  ISBN 0-88946-853-2
  1. Black Muslims. I. Title. II. Series: Studies in religion and
society (New York, N.Y.) ; v. 21.
  BP221.L44 1989
  297' .87--dc19   88-37046

This is volume 21 in the continuing series
Studies in Religion and Society
Volume 21 ISBN 0-88946-853-2
SRS Series ISBN 0-88946-863-X

For information contact **The Edwin Mellen Press**

Box 450   Box 67
Lewiston, New York   Queenston, Ontario
U.S.A. 14092   CANADA L0S 1L0

Mellen House
Lampeter, Dyfed, Wales
UNITED KINGDOM SA48 7DY

Printed in the United States of America

Contents

Acknowledgements

For the help and support they have given me throughout this project, I am indebted to many people. As my M.A. supervisor, Dr. Tom Flanagan was encouraging, patient, and a merciless editor; I am grateful for the guidance he provided. I must also thank Dr. Barry Cooper for his most enlightening concerning the nature of demons, and Nancy Mancell for her valuable assistance in the processing of this manuscript.

The help of the Muslim community and the Nation of Islam was invaluable. Not only did it aid my research, but it made this endeavour a more complete learning experience. I am particularly grateful to Abdul Wali Muhammad and the staff of *The Final Call*, Imam Bilal Muhammad of Toronto, and Imam Nuri Muhammad and the staff of *The Muslim Journal*. I have done my best to interpret the information they shared with me; in no way are they responsible for any errors that may exist in my analysis.

The support of my family is a blessing I have always enjoyed, but it has been truly appreciated during the past two years. This book is dedicated to my parents, Margaret and Frank.

THE NATION OF ISLAM,
AN AMERICAN MILLENARIAN MOVEMENT

INTRODUCTION

... the substance of political society [is] *homonoia* ... spiritual agreement between men; and it is possible between men only in so far as these men live in agreement with the nous, that is, the divinest part in themselves ... Only in so far as men are equal through the love of their noetic self is friendship possible ... [1]

Eric Voegelin

The Black population of the United States has long struggled to find its identity in the context of the society and republic in which it must exist. This struggle is not surprising; the political question "who are we?" must be answered by reflection upon and interpretation of the past. For Black Americans, this process is difficult and painful. Their tie to Africa is undeniable, yet tenuous, and their American origins are rooted in oppression. An answer to this question is necessary, however, for it is the means through which a complete political life may be achieved. As Black Americans know well, slavery is an institution that denies humanity and political visibility. A restoration of their community therefore requires a comprehensive explanation of their origins and an interpretation of the meaning of their existence.

---

[1] Eric Voegelin, *The New Science of Politics*, (Chicago: University of Chicago Press, 1952), p. 77.

One of the most appropriate ways to examine this problem is through religion. Belief in God provides answers to the questions of origin and meaning, and the church a community in which to experience their truth. Not surprisingly, Black Americans have often sought to find a resolution to their plight in theology. It should be noted, however, that man's understanding of the divine is always affected by his experience in the world. While many Blacks found orthodox religious faith to be sufficient, many others stretched its boundaries in order to find an answer that could both explain and affect the political realm.[2] A number of these religious/political groups have emerged, but by far the most successful is the Nation of Islam.[3]

The original doctrine of the Nation provided a cosmology that fit the experience of many Black Americans during the early twentieth century. At its core was millenarianism, the belief in an imminent, ultimate, collective, this-worldly, and total salvation. The White world and its oppressive political institutions would fall; from their ashes would rise the Black millennium. This combination of political and religious symbols served the Muslims well. Individuals were attracted by a doctrine that not only promised a new world, but in many respects seemed to be initiating it. In preparation for the future age, the Nation of Islam rejuvenated the Black family unit, developed an educational system, organized a police force, and acquired vast business holdings. These endeavours lifted the Nation's membership out of the lower class, and established the organization as a permanent institution. Perhaps most importantly, their prophecy of the Fall of America (as the focus of their religious beliefs) fostered a sense of identity and the development of a political

---

[2]See, for example, Arthur Huff Fauset, *Black Gods of the Metropolis, Negro Religious Cults of the Urban North*, (Philadelphia: University of Pennsylvania Press, 1944).

[3]Although the group is commonly referred to as the Black Muslims, that appellation will be avoided here. The Muslims themselves dislike the term, and its use becomes inappropriate after a certain point in their history.

community among Black Americans.

In the following chapters, the history and doctrine of the Nation of Islam will be examined in terms of millenarianism. The sweeping nature of apocalyptic beliefs has made them a suitable field of study for a variety of disciplines. Providing the groundwork for this study, Chapter One considers those theories appropriate to an analysis of the Nation.

Chapter 1

MILLENARIANISM

Then I saw thrones, and seated on them were those to whom judgment was committed. Also I saw the souls of those who had been
beheaded for their testimony to Jesus and for the word of God,
and who had not worshipped the beast or its image and had not
received its mark on their foreheads or their hands. They came to
life, and reigned with Christ for a thousand years.

Revelation 20:4 (RSV)

A comprehensive account of the intricate web that constitutes political
action is perhaps an impossibility; each contribution to its comprehension is
therefore a means by which one can dissect, interpret, and hope to explain
partially. Millenarian theory, which focuses on a particular segment of the
complex weaving together of religion and politics, is an attempt of this kind.
Owing to the nature of its subject, its considerations illuminate a very important type of political action. Essentially, millenarian theory is an analysis
of how and why men envision the perfection of their lives in this world. This
chapter will consider several approaches to millenarianism so as to indicate the

fundamental concepts of this study.

Groups that predict the imminent end of the world seem unimportant, but they are not. Historically, millenarianism has existed both inside established religious and political institutions, and in opposition to them; its effects have ranged from peaceful reform to violent and revolutionary action. As Michael Barkun notes, millenarianism has permitted the continued existence of messianism, influenced major revolutionary upheavals, altered the character of modern social movements, and played a role in the rise of modern totalitarianism.[1] Indeed, it lies at the heart of movements as diverse and important as Christianity and Marxism. The complexity of the concept is reflected in the number and variety of works that have attempted to understand and explain it. Millenarianism has been studied by scholars from disciplines as diverse as political science, theology, history, psychology, anthropology, and sociology.

The term millennium, from *mille* meaning one thousand and *annus* meaning year, is derived from a prophetic passage in the Book of Revelation, and implies the concept of a chosen people and their rise, through God's grace, to a thousand-year reign of glory.[2]

Yonina Talmon has noted that there are five common characteristics of the vision of salvation that emerge from this basic idea. The millennium will be: (1) collective, in that salvation will be shared by the faithful, (2) this-worldly, in that the transformation will occur on this earth, (3) imminent, in that it will occur soon, likely within the believers' lifetime, (4) ultimate, in that

---

[1] Michael Barkun, *Disaster and the Millennium*, (New Haven: Yale University Press, 1974), p. 21.

[2] In modern scholarship the qualification of the millennium as being one thousand years long is interpreted loosely, often referring to any ultimate period of bliss. Examples of this usage can be found in Michael Barkun's *Disaster and the Millennium*, and Peter Worsley's *The Trumpet Shall Sound*, (London: Paladin Books, 1970).

the change will bring about the final state of being in history, and (5) total, in that the world will become the incarnation of perfection.[3] Such a belief completely transforms the meaning of its adherents' existence in history. It is thus qualitatively different from normal political and religious affiliations, and its power is undeniable. If primarily religious, millenarian beliefs can easily expand into the political sphere. If originally political, the hope and fervour necessitated by an imminent millennium can move them closer to the religious sphere.

With their promise of a perfect future, millenarian visions are particularly appealing to the poor and oppressed. Talmon writes that the primary cause of the development of millenarianism is multiple deprivation, the lack of a variety of societal goods.[4] Groups near the bottom of the social order suffer in many ways. Poverty-stricken, politically powerless, and unable to climb the social ladder, they suffer profound feelings of deprivation and resentment. By themselves, these feelings might not be sufficient to inspire action. When combined, they may move a group to seek an alternative future. The "myth of the elect" and "role reversals"[5] of millenarianism are an effective means of alleviating this pain.

The concept of relative deprivation has also been used to understand millenarianism. By relative deprivation is meant that even when ghettoized, social outcasts must still live within the context of a larger population of comparatively privileged individuals. The gap between these groups thus appears as a relative proportion. The larger the gap, the smaller the chance it will ever be reconciled, and the greater the frustration of the deprived group.

---

[3]Yonina Talmon, "Millenarism," in *The International Encyclopedia of the Social Sciences,* Vol. 10, (Macmillan and Co., 1968), p. 351.

[4]Yonina Talmon, "Millenarism," p. 354.

[5]*Ibid.*

Talmon also suggests that millenarianism may emerge from the search for "a coherent value system," a new cultural identity, and "a regained sense of dignity and self-respect." [6] In the attempt to give itself status by creating a separate identity, a group can easily adopt millenarian beliefs; apocalyptic expectations often involve the idea of a Chosen People, as well as a code of accepted behaviour.

In his article "Revitalization Movements," Anthony Wallace examines this idea in detail. Wallace interprets beliefs such as millenarianism as a means by which a culture can be revitalized.[7] Societies, like living organisms, attempt to maintain homeostasis. Under stress, the community must adjust to survive. Revitalization movements allow an adjustment of the society's mazeway, or worldview. Wallace argues that altering their mazeways allows endangered societies to continue. The stress upon communities is constant, and they must therefore always be at some stage in the reformulation of their mazeway. This pattern forms a cycle;[8] millenarian movements, as part of this cycle, can be expected to reoccur in a specific society or group.

The internal qualities of a group are important in the development of millenarian beliefs, but so too is the character of society as a whole. In his book *Disaster and the Millennium*, Michael Barkun contends that in any society, disaster is a necessary catalyst for the development of millenarian movements.[9]

Barkun states that not only must a society be "primed" for creating a millenarian movement, but the movement must be jarred into existence by a

---

[6]Yonina Talmon, "Millenarism," p. 355.

[7]Anthony Wallace, "Revitalization Movements," *American Anthropologist*, 58 (1956), p. 265.

[8]The cycle Wallace outlines is as follows: (1) steady state, (2) increased individual stress, (3) cultural distortion, and (4) revitalization. *Ibid.*, pp. 268-71.

[9]Barkun defines disaster as "a severe, relatively sudden, and frequently unexpected disruption of normal structural arrangements within a social system, or subsystem ... over which the system has no control." Michael Barkun, *Disaster and the Millennium*, p. 51.

period of societal shock. According to him, after a community has undergone a number of disasters, it will suffer "disaster syndrome," a condition he describes as "a reaction to disaster characterized by non-rational behavior." [10] This syndrome, a combination of sensory deprivation and overstimulation, causes a high level of susceptibility. Increased stress results in decreased mental efficiency, information processing abilities, and critical abilities. The community can no longer cope with its environment.

Barkun hypothesizes that there are three possible patterns of response when a society undergoes such a trauma. The first is apathy and decay; a society may simply give up. As examples Barkun cites the Minoans, Etruscans, and Mayans. The second response he terms defensive structuring, "... the establishment of mechanisms which ... neutralize the effects of external stress ..." [11] This reaction occurs when the primary threat is to cultural identity, rather than physical survival.[12]

The third possible response to disaster syndrome is millenarianism. The social fabric from which it emerges is characterized by the interaction of "appropriate cultural motifs," charismatic leadership, and community isolation. Nearly any type of severe and repetitive disaster can foster its development, but Barkun finds four situations that will not yield this response. They are: (1) those that leave most of the original environment intact, (2) those where the damage is quickly repaired, (3) those which are prolonged within the same social unit, and (4), those which occur in the absence of ideas regarding fu-

---

[10]Michael Barkun, *Disaster and the Millennium*, p. 52. Although one major disaster may cause disaster syndrome, it is far more likely to develop after a series of disasters has occurred.

[11]*Ibid.*, p. 77.

[12]Barkun adds that defensive structuring often "marks the conclusion" of millenarian movements. When the millennium fails to occur, group members resort to more realistic means to adapt to their environment.

ture change. [13] These types of catastrophes leave too much of the original environment and "mazeway" intact to warrant a complete reconstruction.

An outline of theories regarding the origins of millenarian movements would not be complete without the inclusion of Bernard McGinn's *Visions of the End.* McGinn presents a specific criticism of Cohn's *The Pursuit of the Millennium.* It is his contention that Cohn neglected the role of millenarianism, or apocalypticism, in the established Church.[14] McGinn studies roughly the same period as Cohn, but he presents what is best described as a history of theological change rather than a history of the Church and its associated institutions. McGinn divides the period of early apocalypticism into two ages: (1) Classical Apocalypticism (200 B.C. to A.D. 100), evidenced most clearly in the pattern of communal crisis, judgment, and salvation, found in typical Jewish prophetic literature of the period, and (2), Patristic Apocalypticism (A.D. 100-400), which stresses the Christian belief in a personal afterlife and a concern for the eschatological meaning of the present, rather than for the future.[15] According to McGinn, the central function of apocalypticism is that it permits men to locate themselves in history, specifically in their relationship to eternity.

All millenarian doctrines by implication contain an evaluation of the society in which they must exist, and the way in which followers interpret the evil of the present world determines what must be done to achieve the millennium. In *Magic and the Millennium*, Bryan Wilson provides a typology that aids interpretation of this aspect of millennialism. Wilson's categories are based upon the way groups view evil and the soteriological theories that develop from this

---

[13]Michael Barkun,*Disaster and the Millennium*, p. 64.

[14]Bernard McGinn, *Visions of the End*, (New York: Columbia University Press, 1979), p. 29.

[15]*Ibid.*, pp. 2-15.

fundamental belief. While no one classification is adequate to describe fully a particular group, his method of analysis provides a convenient system for considering the saving myths of most political and religious millenarians. Wilson's typology accounts for seven basic responses: (1) Conversionist, wherein the world is interpreted as corrupt because men are corrupt; if men can be changed, the world will be changed; (2) Revolutionist, wherein the destruction of the world, both natural and social, is required to save men; (3) Introversionist, wherein man's complete withdrawal from the world is necessary to save him; (4) Manipulationist, which requires that men adopt or learn a new way of interpreting evil; (5)Thaumaturgical, wherein salvation is achieved in a personal form by specific personal acts; (6) Reformist, which requires an alteration in social organization for salvation to occur; and finally, (7), Utopian, wherein the world must be reconstructed to eliminate evil completely.[16] A specific group might contain fragments of each of Wilson's categories or through its history might touch on all of them. His typology is, for the study of millenarianism, a flexible reference with which it is possible to analyze content, rather than a strict methodology for categorization.

A number of authors have attempted to categorize millenarian beliefs. Michael Barkun and Peter Worsley, for example, divide millenarian movements into two distinct categories: passive and active. For both, passive movements are those that have either: (1) confronted society or a failed millennium and continued to exist, or (2) those that view the millennium as brought about by a distant God or inevitable history.[17] Activist movements are those that view themselves as playing a role in the initiation of the millennium. (For Wors-

---

[16]Bryan Wilson, *Magic and the Millennium*, (New York: Harvard University Press, 1973), pp. 22-30.

[17]Michael Barkun, *Disaster and the Millennium*, p. 19, and Peter Worsley, *The Trumpet Shall Sound*, pp. 239-44.

ley, both forms eventually must develop into secular political organizations or fade away.)[18] Vittorio Lanternari discusses a similar categorization. He argues that the division exists, but that it is based on the type of conflict that the millenarian group is facing. Intercultural clash yields a salvation achieved by immediate action and militant struggle, while endogenous movements "look for salvation through spiritual, cultural, or ethical channels ..."[19] Although this division fits well with Lanternari's thesis, it is not completely accurate. The Nation of Islam, medieval Christianity, and the early Pai Maire movement of which Michael Adas writes,[20] all illustrate the limited applicability of his theory. While Barkun and Worsley's classification therefore appears the more acceptable, it too runs into difficulty. Barkun himself notes that it is often difficult to distinguish groups who are attempting to "force the end" from groups who view themselves as merely making "prudent preparations."[21] "Prudent preparations," as Barkun writes, "may themselves wreak social havoc."[22] Like Wilson's classification, the active/passive dichotomy ought to be applied only in a general sense, and then only with caution.

Millenarian visions vary across groups, but there is one feature common to all of them. Michael Adas, in *Prophets of Rebellion*, states that for millenarians there is no true dichotomy between past and present.[23] Their vision, although often a supernatural gift, is to some degree always based on their experience

---

[18]Peter Worsley, *The Trumpet Shall Sound*, p. 244.

[19]Vittorio Lanternari, *Religions of the Oppressed*, Trans. L. Sergio, (New York: Mentor Books Ltd., 1965), p. 247.

[20]Michael Adas, *Prophets of Rebellion*, (Chapel Hill: University of North Carolina Press, 1979), p. 17.

[21]Michael Barkun, *Disaster and the Millennium*, p. 19.

[22]*Ibid.*

[23]Michael Adas, *Prophets of Rebellion*, (Chapel Hill: University of North Carolina Press, 1979), p. xxvi.

of the past and their existence in a specific environment. Striking examples of this can be found in the writings of Karl Marx and Edward Bellamy. The former based his writings upon what appeared to be a firmly entrenched dichotomy of bourgeoisie and proletariat, while the idealized future of the latter contained anachronistic technology based upon his own experiences in the nineteenth century. Millenarianism can reflect this fact in more subtle ways as well. Peter Worsley adds to the theoretical analysis of millenarianism an appreciation for this subtlety. In his study of Melanesian tribes and their reaction to the arrival of Whites, Worsley discusses the millennial vision held by participants in New Guinea's Vailala Madness. Intertwining history, cultural shock, and tribal myth, the native islanders merged their cyclical view of time with the Christian missionaries' linear interpretation. Dead ancestors, rather than returning through a process of reincarnation, were instead thought to be the White colonists who sailed into their harbours.[24] The ordering of the Islanders' world had been fundamentally altered, and this precipitated the formation of a complex millennium. The vision of perfection in which millenarians place their hope is thus never an isolated creation.

The attempt to classify millenarian visions is an ambitious project; indeed, few authors have attempted it. In *Disaster and the Millennium*, however, Michael Barkun provides a scheme for categorizing millenarian movements of the twentieth century; he finds them to be of three types. The first category is "classical movements," those which conform to the pattern of medieval rural millenarianism, but do so in an urban setting. He includes in this group such movements as the Nation of Islam. Barkun's second category is that of pan-national millenarianism, doctrines that encompass some idea of messianic nationalism, for example the Rastafari cult of Jamaica. The third category of

---

[24]Peter Worsley, *The Trumpet Shall Sound*, (London: Paladin Books, 1970, pp. 90-91.

belief that Barkun delineates is totalitarianism, a form of millenarianism best exemplified by National Socialism.[25] Although this framework is an admirable attempt to classify millenarian visions, an important but avoided aspect of millenarian scholarship, it is not completely accurate. It is likely that most groups will fall between these categories or share several of their attributes. The Nation of Islam, for example, can be interpreted as pan-national in character, while its prophesied millennium can be seen as totalitarian.

Perhaps the most fascinating issue in the study of millenarianism is the consideration of the meaning of these movements within society. Two very different schools of interpretation have attempted to answer this question. The first and more traditional view is that of theorists such as Norman Cohn and Eric Voegelin. These thinkers interpret millenarian movements as a form of spiritual sickness. The second, more recent interpretation of these groups is evidenced in the work of Peter Worsley and Vittorio Lanternari. For these authors, millenarianism is is the final pre-political stage of a community. It is a means to deal with societal pressures and problems in the present, and a mechanism through which a community can improve and better organize itself to function in the future.

In *The Pursuit of the Millennium*, Norman Cohn examines millenarian groups from early Christianity to John of Leyden. In considering their history, he finds that the vast majority sprang up from what can best be referred to as the rootless poor. The process of industrialization and urbanization which occurred in medieval Europe created a large population of homeless, poverty-

---

[25]In *The Hitler Movement – A Modern Millenarian Revolution*, (Stanford: Hoover Institute Press, 1980), James Rhodes provides a detailed theoretical analysis of Hitler's National Socialist movement. It is notable both for its detailed research and documentation, and for its analysis of the dual structure of millenarian movements; Rhodes considers the beliefs of membership as well as leadership. This book is one of the first modern case studies to integrate the work of Michael Barkun and Norman Cohn.

stricken individuals. Such individuals found hope and fulfillment in a set of ideas that promised them a rule of eternal glory. For Cohn, however, these millenarian myths of collective supremacy and meaning in history combine to overpower any redemptive effects the belief system might have. Millenarianism is a form of spiritual illness, to use Eric Voegelin's term, a pneumopathological disorder. Voegelin writes:

> ... an immanentist hypostasis of the eschaton ... is a theoretical fallacy ... history has no *eidos* ... The meaning of history, thus, is an illusion; and this illusory *eidos* is created by treating a symbol of faith as if it were a proposition concerning an object of immanent experience.[26]

The Pursuit of the Millennium closes with a warning regarding modern revolutionary millenarianism and self-divinization, and it is clear that this caution stems from Cohn's concern over the rise of Communism and National Socialism in Europe.[27] Bringing a spiritual belief into the immanent world often yields totalitarianism. For Cohn, every millenarian movement holds this potential.

Norman Cohn and Eric Voegelin's interpretation of millenarianism stems from their ability to understand millenarians as they understand themselves. Although neither theorist finds benefit in such beliefs, their respect for myth allows them a clear vision of millenarianism in the context of a political community.

This same method of analysis is adopted by Yonina Talmon, but she adds to Cohn's theoretical outline the idea that millenarianism often emerges from

---

[26]Eric Voegelin, *The New Science of Politics*, (Chicago: University of Chicago Press, 1952), p. 120.

[27]Norman Cohn, *The Pursuit of the Millennium*, p. 286.

the search for a new identity and/or a new "value system."[28] This aspect of millenarianism is evidenced both in Hitler's Germany, where the ideal Aryan became a new identity, and in the Nation of Islam where a restorative identity was a fundamental tenet of the group's doctrine. It is from the differences such as exist between these groups that the division in millenarian scholarship arises. While the collective identity and "value system" of the Germans under Hitler were clearly pathological, the role of the Nation of Islam's new Black Man appears more ambiguous. It is possible to interpret their achievement as a creative and healthy response to a social problem. Two authors of the early 1960s discuss this facet of millenarianism.

Vittorio Lanternari, in *Religions of the Oppressed,* and Peter Worsley in *The Trumpet Shall Sound,* present an international survey of millenarian movements. Through their work, a second interpretation of millenarianism is illuminated: that of millennial movements as a functional mechanism.

The theory underlying this position is perhaps best discussed by Worsley. Like Cohn, he finds millenarianism to be most prevalent in the lower classes, but he does not see its developmental process in the same light. For Worsley, there is no direct transition from medieval millenarianism to totalitarianism. After the Reformation, he states, most millennial movements in Europe became passive and were associated with the most backward elements of society.[29]

With reference to the Melanesian islanders he studied in detail, Worsley outlines three types of societies from which he sees millenarianism developing. In his categorization, it is possible to discern the influence of Marxist theory.

The first quality that Worsley specifies as characteristic of populations wherein millennialism arises is that they are often

---

[28] Yonina Talmon, "Millenarism," p. 355.

[29] Peter Worsley, *The Trumpet Shall Sound,* p. 233.

> ... divided into small, separate narrow and isolated social units ... [and]
> occur, firstly, among people living in the so-called 'stateless' soci-
> eties, societies which have no overall unity, which lack centralized
> political institutions, and which may lack specialized political in-
> stitutions altogether.[30]

Millenarianism is the vehicle through which individuals may organize themselves against a common enemy. Achieving their first political identity through
recognition of the enemy, these social units require a means to express that
identity. Millennialism can bring together previously hostile groups in this
manner. As the cult is partly religious in nature, leaders can appeal to the
supernatural and thereby appear to transcend sectional interests. In this way
millenarian movements integrate and organize the population.

A second situation Worsley sees as conducive to the development of millenarianism is the agrarian or feudal state. Using Marx's theoretical analysis
of the French Peasants (from the "Eighteenth Brumaire of Louis Bonaparte"),
he equates social organization with the stateless society discussed above. Here
too, the cult serves an integratory function. A millenarian movement effectively gathers together those with similar interests.

The third set of conditions Worsley finds conducive to millenarian movements occur when a particular society's basis is destroyed or in danger of being
destroyed.[31] In this type of situation, people may unite in order to save their
community. Millenarian movements, usually in part political, and carrying
with them a religious remnant of the culture to be saved, are a useful and appropriate way of attempting to fight that threat. They are a means by which
one's culture can be "revitalized."

---

[30]Peter Worsley, *The Trumpet Shall Sound*, p. 235.

[31]*Ibid.*, pp. 235-45.

Worsley closes his argument with an hypothesis regarding the future of millenarian movements in Melanesia; he believes that in the future radical millenarians will become increasingly political, eventually becoming completely secularized. In the development of a society, millennial beliefs are thus a transitional phase. As Lanternari writes, they

> ... serve to implement the popular awareness of the need for change
> in the religious life, and, in so doing, pave the way for reform in
> the cultural, political, and social structure of secular society.[32]

By redefining morality and acceptable social behaviour, and by changing a community's interpretation of both itself and history, millenarianism functions as a means to develop society. It is in this sense that the functional interpretation of millenarianism is Marxist in nature. It stresses that societies progress in a pre-determined pattern, and in so doing, denies the independent validity of religious experience.[33] In essence, functional interpretations of millenarianism impose an external order and meaning upon a group's myths and history.

Fueled by the energy and zeal of a desperate people, and embodying all hope they have for the future, a millenarian prophecy is at all times extremely volatile. As the expected time of the apocalypse draws closer, the believers' faith becomes more intense, and their actions more completely directed towards a single vision of the future. No great eschatological culmination of history has yet occurred, however; one important question thus arises. What is to be done when the millennium does not arrive?

The history of millenarian groups indicates that there are three common responses to the failure of prophecy. An unyielding reality may cause indi-

---

[32]Vittorio Lanternari, *The Religions of the Oppressed*, p. 254.

[33]This point is also argued with respect to Worsley by Michael Barkun, but not on the basis of its Marxist origins.

viduals to leave the group, or conversely, may cause them to proselytize with greater urgency than ever before. A third alternative is the reinterpretation and/or de-eschatologizing of the group's doctrine.

Somewhat surprisingly, it is rare for millenarians to completely desert their beliefs. This fact becomes understandable when the nature of millenarian beliefs is considered. As noted above, millennialism is markedly different from other political and religious affiliations. It reinterprets a community's past and present, insuring a glorious future. Individuals invest not only time and money into millenarianism, but also their heart and soul. This investment is often too great to be abandoned.

A more common response to the disconfirmation of prophecy is an increased fervency of belief. *When Prophecy Fails*, (by Leon Festinger, Henry Riecken, and Stanley Schachter), is a detailed examination of the development of a millenarian group from its inception to its demise. The uniqueness of this study makes it unlikely that any other case study could duplicate its results. For this reason, *When Prophecy Fails* has been used as a theoretical basis for research in cognitive dissonance rather than a falsifiable experiment in the sociology of groups.

Festinger and others contend that a failed prophecy causes an "important and painful dissonance"[34] for believers; an individual's beliefs and experience of reality conflict. Because millenarian beliefs affect many aspects of an adherent's life, this dissonance cannot be ignored or denied. Believers will instead actively attempt to reduce it. An effective means of achieving this is to convince others of their ideas, for

If more and more people can be persuaded that the system of belief

---

[34]Leon Festinger; Henry Riecken; Stanley Schachter; *When Prophecy Fails*, (New York: Harper Torchbooks, 1966), p. 27.

is correct, then clearly it must, after all, be correct. [35]

Rather than changing their internal belief system, adherents attempt to alter the outside world. Festinger and others found five conditions necessary for this process to occur: (1) a belief held with conviction, (2) a strong commitment to that belief, (3) a thorough disconfirmation of that belief must be possible, (4) such disconfirmation must undeniably occur, and (5) social support must be available following that disconfirmation.[36] If these conditions are met, and the internal condition of the group is stable, members can then begin the process of adjusting the outside environment through proselytizing. If this activity is successful, cognitive dissonance will be reduced, and the group and its beliefs can continue to exist. An example of this type of behaviour can be found in the actions of Louis Riel, who "redoubled his evangelistic efforts"[37] after the failure of his prophecy and his subsequent surrender to the police.

The research of Festinger and others has been the basis for a great deal of work in the field of social psychology. Its common sense appeal and the appropriateness of its concepts have seen it used in studies of many millenarian groups as well. Robert Carroll, in his book *When Prophecy Failed*, presents a critique of the theory and its applicability to millenarianism. He argues that while cognitive dissonance theory is a useful way of examining millenarian groups, it is also limited in many respects, and therefore should be used with caution.

Carroll's first criticism concerns a point that can be considered both an advantage and a disadvantage: the vague nature of much of Festinger's terminology.[38]

---

[35]Leon Festinger; Henry Rieken; Stanley Schachter; *When Prophecy Fails*, p. 28.

[36]*Ibid.*, p. 21.

[37]Thomas Flanagan, "The Mission of Louis Riel," *Alberta History*, Vol. 23, 1973, p. 5.

[38]Robert Carroll, *When Prophecy Failed, Reactions and Responses to Failure in the Old Prophetic Traditions*, (London: SCM Press Ltd., 1979), p. 104.

Supporters of cognitive dissonance theory contend this vagueness is in part responsible for the vast amount of research that the theory has generated. While this is partly true, the fact remains that vague terminology also serves to reduce the richness of explanation a theory provides. Carroll quotes R. Brown regarding this point. He describes Festinger's terminology and definitions as "imprecise hodgepodges of logic, grammar, and common-sense cognitive psychology."[39] In particular, Carroll questions the vague definitions of the terms cognition and drive. The former he feels is defined too broadly, while the latter indicates either the reduction of psychology to biology, or else a mere analogy.[40]

A more fundamental criticism Carroll makes of cognitive dissonance theory is its assumption that dissonance must move the sufferer to eliminate it; other researchers have suggested that the tolerance of dissonance can be considered a valuable ability. John Keats felt that such "negative capabilities" helped individuals to cope in times of stress,[41] while Paul Halmos has suggested that rather than attempting to entirely block out reality, individuals attempt to maintain a "dissonance equilibration," a condition he defines as:

> ... an oscillation of preference which tries to maintain a state of equilibrium between opposites rather than seeking to obliterate the problem.[42]

The feasibility of these two alternatives indicates again that caution must be exercised in the application of cognitive dissonance theory.

---

[39]R. Brown, *Social Psychology*, (New York: 1975), p. 595, as cited in Robert Carroll, *When Prophecy Failed*, p. 104.

[40]Robert Carroll, *When Prophecy Failed*, pp. 104-5.

[41]*Ibid.*, p. 104.

[42]*Ibid.*

Perhaps the most important criticism Carroll makes of the application of cognitive dissonance theory to millenarianism concerns the nature of religious prophecy itself. Quite simply, it is often difficult to assess exactly what constitutes its failure. For religious millenarians, prophecy is the gift of a transcendent, superior being; the possiblity therefore exists that earthly adherents honestly misinterpreted a complicated message, or that the message-giver changed his mind. [43] Indeed, the Jehovah's Witnesses have sometimes made use of these types of explanation.[44]

Another important element of dissonance theory is the recognition by adherents that a disconfirmation has occurred. Carroll notes that often a belief may be held so strongly that disconfirming evidence may simply go unrecognized.

> The nature of hope for the future is such that it can hardly be falsified by any amount of apparent disconfirmation ... Aspects of that hope may have been damaged by the passage of time ... but hope itself is a far more resilient force and will have provided a constant resource for overcoming temporary setbacks.[45]

Because this criticism encompasses groups that by definition do not suffer cognitive dissonance, it must be interpreted as a limitation of theory's scope rather than of its applicability. Relying solely on Festinger's definition of failed prophecy limits the types of beliefs and believers one may consider.

Robert Carroll's critique of cognitive dissonance theory stands as a caution against whole-hearted acceptance of a social science theory in a field that is in

---

[43]Robert Carroll, *When Prophecy Failed*, pp. 112-13.

[44]J.F. Zygmunt, "Prophetic Failure and Chiliastic Identity: The Case of Jehovah's Witnesses," *American Journal of Sociology* 75 (1970), p. 934.

[45]Robert Carroll, *When Prophecy Failed*, p. 115.

part theological. Carroll himself makes use of the theory in his study of Old Testament prophecy, but unlike Festinger and others, he finds the development of a hermeneutic to be the most prevalent response to failure of prophecy:

> ... the experience of dissonance force[s] individuals or groups to reinterpret their basic material or the contemporary events so as to avoid dissonance. [46]

Reinterpretation may follow any number of routes: the millennium may be pushed further into the future, interpreted as only partially fulfilled, or history itself may be reinterpreted. Exemplifying this form of response are the Jehovah's Witnesses; Zygmunt notes that in the past, prophesied dates for the millennium's arrival have usually been interpreted as a time during which partial fulfillment of a prophecy occurred.[47] This method of understanding the failure of prophecy is not entirely secure, however. It does not account completely for the experienced failure, and frequently merely posits another date for the millennium's arrival; the possibility therefore exists that the group may be disappointed again. In his work *Evolution and Christian Hope*, Ernst Benz discusses a similar, but more effective response to the failure of prophecy: de-eschatologizing.

Benz provides an analysis of the influence of eschatology on Church doctrine and philosophy from the beginnings of Christianity to the writings of Teilhard de Chardin. In his discussion of St. Augustine the concept of de-eschatologizing is well illustrated.

The early Christian church was explicitly millennial; members anticipated an imminent and triumphal return of Christ. As time passed, however, the

---

[46]Robert Carroll, *When Prophecy Failed*, p. 210.

[47]J.F. Zygmunt, "Prophetic Failure and Chiliastic Identity: The Case of Jehovah's Witnesses," pp. 933-35.

truth of this prediction was called into question. At the same time, the faith came to be an established institution of the Roman Empire, a role wherein millenarian tendencies were unacceptable. The continued existence of the Church therefore depended upon a reinterpretation of the original doctrine. St. Augustine accomplished this feat through de-eschatologizing, a process Benz defines as "the removal of the original basic attitude toward the end of time in the gospel message."[48] Essentially, Augustine's interpretation emphasized the Catholic Church as the embodiment of the Kingdom of God on earth.

> The *first resurrection* is not connected any more with the coming of the Last Judgement at the end of time, but rather with the Church. It is the revival of the spirits who were condemned to hell and death. By their faith in the Gospel of the Church, they are revived to a life of bliss... it affects the spirit and is consumated in baptism. The *second resurrection* affects the body and is accomplished at the end of time when Christ returns for the Last Judgement.[49]

Benz refers to this process as a form of "ecclesiastical positivism,"[50] and it can be seen as a parallel of Voegelin's "immanentization of the eschaton."[51] While in its purely religious form such a theoretical transformation is perhaps not quite as dangerous as totalitarianism or communism, taken to the extreme, it can yield similar results. This self-interpretation of the Catholic Church was perhaps responsible for its evolution into a highly politicized institution.

Augustine's thought permitted the Church's transition from a radical millenarian sect into a formal and permanent institution. A doctrine of revolution

---

[48]Ernst Benz, *Evolution and Christian Hope*, Trans. H.G. Frank, (Garden City: Anchor Books, 1968), p. 23.

[49]*Ibid.*, p. 26.

[50]*Ibid.*

[51]Eric Voegelin, *The New Science of Politics*, p. 139.

became a doctrine of institutionalized power. The existence of an original un-altered text allowed millenarianism to surface again, however, as with Joachim of Fiore. The latter's connection of theology with progress is echoed in the writings of Darwin, Marx, and Nietzsche.

The Nation of Islam's doctrine of the Fall of America is clearly millenar-ian, and throughout the organization's history, these eschatological beliefs have influenced the Muslims' political and religious actions. Elijah Muhammad orig-inally prophesied the apocalypse for the years 1965 and 1966;[52] its "failure" to occur during that period saw the Muslims utilize many of the adaptive mech-anisms discussed above, for example, reinterpretation and de-eschatologizing. The following chapters will concentrate on these responses and examine their effect on the Nation's doctrine and history.

---

[52]Elijah Muhammad, *The Message to the Blackman in America*, (Chicago: Muhammad Mosque of Islam No. 2, 1965), p. 270.

Chapter 2

EARLY HISTORY AND DOCTRINE

The years 1965 and 1966 are going to be fateful for America, bringing in the "Fall of America" ... This is the setting of the nations for a showdown to determine who will live on earth. The survivor is to build a nation of peace to rule the people forever under the guidance of Almighty God, Allah.[1]

Elijah Muhammad

During the Great Depression, the urban ghettos of the northern United States were fertile ground for the development of new religious movements. Between 1900 and 1930 approximately 2,250,000 Blacks left the rural south; most emigrated to large northern cities.[2] This growth represented an increase of over 400 percent in the Black population of the north; in Detroit, the increase

---

[1]Elijah Muhammad, *The Message to the Blackman in America*, (Chicago: Muhammad's Mosque of Islam No. 2, 1965), p. 270.

[2]C.E. Lincoln, *The Black Muslims in America*, Rev. Ed., (Boston: Beacon Press, 1973), p. xxiii.

exceeded 611 percent. [3]

The industrialized north had been viewed by many as a land of abundance, holding the promise of a better standard of living, employment, and equality. Most Blacks however, suffered severe economic hardship during this period. Their sense of deprivation was intensified by the difficulty of adjusting to a new environment and inequalities they endured in the social realm.

Economic pressure often moves individuals to focus on their religious faith with greater urgency, and in the ghettos this tendency not surprisingly took on political overtones. Blacks were beginning to emerge from the shadow of slavery, and their religion had, of necessity, always served a variety of functions. Indeed, Fauset hypothesized that Black Americans' traditionally high religious participation was in part the result of the lack of other channels open to them.[4] His research suggests that religious movements provided Black Americans the opportunity to participate

in an atmosphere free from embarassment or apology, [they are] a place where they may experiment in activities such as business, politics, social reform, and social expression.[5]

As well, he maintained that participation was often motivated by a racial or nationalistic urge.[6] The absolute and relative deprivation suffered by Blacks during the Depression would have exaggerated these tendencies on a large scale. The first groups to crystallize out of this initial ferment were the Moorish Science Temple, led by Noble Drew Ali, and the Universal Negro Improvement Association (U.N.I.A.) of Marcus Garvey.

---

[3]C.E. Lincoln, *The Black Muslims in America*, Rev. Ed., pp. xxiii-xxiv.

[4]A. Huff Fauset, *Black Gods of the Metropolis, Negro Religious Cults of the Urban North*, (Philadelphia: University of Pennsylvania Press, 1944), p. 107.

[5]*Ibid.*, pp. 107-8.

[6]*Ibid.*, p. 121.

The Moorish Science Temple originated in 1913.[7] Its leader, Noble Drew
Ali, preached a doctrine that included a strict moral code and linked religion
to nationality:

> Christianity is for the European (paleface); Moslemism is for the
> Asiatic (olive-skinned). When each group has its own peculiar re-
> ligion, there will be peace on earth.[8]

Salvation depended upon accepting a new nationality: followers became Moors.
Although its central tenets were undeniably political, the group did not take
political action. They stressed obedience and loyalty to the American flag,
believed divine intervention would bring about the end of white rule, and
therefore cultivated an apolitical, peaceful adherence to the *status quo.* [9] The
primarily religious Moorish Science Temple did, however, initiate overt political statements on the part of Black religion and laid the foundation for the
movements that followed it. Noble Drew Ali's death saw the Temple virtually
disappear; in its place, a more political group emerged.

The Universal Negro Improvement Association originated in 1916 and was
perhaps the most popular "back to Africa" movement in American history. The
Garveyites, as they were known, invested their money and energy into amass-
ing a large commercial empire, the goal of which was to see Africa become the
homeland of all Blacks.[10] Like the Nation of Islam (which later developed from
it), the U.N.I.A. stressed Black independence through self-sufficiency. Indeed,
Marcus Garvey himself originated the phrase "Up, you mighty race, you can

---

[7]C.E. Lincoln, *The Black Muslims in America*, p. 53.

[8]J.M. Yinger, *Religion, Society and the Individual,* (New York: The Macmillan Co., 1957),
p. 504, as quoted in C.E. Lincoln, *The Black Muslims in America*, p. 56.

[9]C.E. Lincoln, *The Black Muslims in America*, p. 57.

[10]*Ibid*, p. 62.

accomplish what you will," [11] a rallying cry frequently used by the Muslims' Messenger Elijah Muhammad. The movement progressed to the point of electing a Liberian government-in-exile, even having its own representative to the League of Nations, but began to lose momentum when the President of Liberia understandably refused the U.N.I.A. entry to his country.[12] Marcus Garvey was exiled in 1927 and his movement then faded from prominence.[13]

The waning of these two groups left a void in Black religious/political life at precisely the time such a channel was needed most. The Great Depression, a disaster of momentous proportions, loomed on the horizon. This void was filled by the Nation of Islam.

Wallace D. Fard,[14] later interpreted by members of his movement as Allah, or the Great Mahdi incarnate, first appeared in Detroit in July of 1930. Little is known of his early life and his founding of the Nation of Islam; the information that does exist is vague and often contradictory. For his followers, this mystery adds to his aura of divinity.

Despite their dislike of Caucasians, members of the Nation of Islam acknowledge that the mother of the pale-skinned Fard was white:

> He said his father went often in the mountains there in their country
> where some Caucasians were living. (They think that they are
> Moslems and they do think that they are Christians or they belong
> to the Christians too.) He said he got one of these women and

---

[11]C.E. Lincoln, *The Black Muslims in America*, p. 61.

[12]*Ibid.*

[13]It has not completely disappeared however. Currently, Garvey's organization is called the United Afro-American Improvement Association. Interview with Imam Bilal Muhammad, Toronto, January 3, 1986.

[14]Wallace Fard used a variety of names. C.E. Lincoln lists a number of them: Farrad Mohammad, Mr. F. Mohammad Ali, and Professor Ford. C.E. Lincoln, *The Black Muslims in America*, p. 14. In recent years, the Muslims have come to refer to him as Farad.

took her for his wife so he could get a son to live more like this civilization of the whites so as to be able to get among them and they will not be able to distinguish him ...[15]

Complementary myths concerning Fard's ethnic origins are diverse. In his classic work on the movement, C.E. Lincoln notes that among them is a legend that describes Fard as a black Jamaican whose father was a Syrian Moslem, and one that reports he was a Palestinian with a long history of participating in racial agitations.[16] In terms of the role Fard was eventually to play in the Nation's theology, two of these myths stand out. To Elijah Muhammad (later the leader of the Movement), he declared himself a member of the royal dynasty of the Hashimide Sheriffs of Mecca, while to Elijah's wife Clara, he apparently stated he was a member of the tribe of Koreish (the prophet Mohammad's tribe).[17] Both of these claims gave Fard added legitimacy in the eyes of his followers.[18]

Initially, Fard spread his religious message while selling silks door-to-door. Although an unusual method of proselytizing, it was effective. His doctrine rapidly gained followers; their meetings were at first held in private homes, but soon the group was able to rent a meeting hall for their Temple. Within three years Fard developed a cohesive organization that included an elementary school for Muslim children, the University of Islam, training classes for women

---

[15]Transcript of an interview with Elijah Muhammad. Hatim A. Sahib, *The Nation of Islam*, (Master's Thesis, University of Chicago, 1951), p. 94.

[16]C.E. Lincoln, *The Black Muslims in America*, p. 14.

[17]Hatim A. Sahib, *The Nation of Islam*, p. 69.

[18]Perhaps with this goal too, Fard also at one point claimed to be the reincarnation of Noble Drew Ali. C.E. Marsh, *From Black Muslims to Muslims: The Transition from Separatism to Islam*, (Metuchen: Scarecrow Press, Inc., 1984), p. 51. The Muslims' connection with Noble Drew Ali and Marcus Garvey was also assumed by Elijah Muhammad, later the movement's leader. He referred to the two men as "fine Muslims." E.U. Essien-Udom, *Black Nationalism*, (Chicago: University of Chicago Press, 1961), p. 63.

on how to be proper wives and mothers, the Muslim Girls Training Class, and a private security force, the Fruit of Islam. [19]

Early in the development of the Nation, Wallace Fard attracted a man who was to become the organization's most important convert: Elijah Poole. The poverty-stricken son of a "Jack leg" preacher, Poole had come to Detroit in 1923, hoping to make a better life for himself and his family.[20] Like many other Blacks, he soon discovered life in the north was no better than it had been in the south. Uncertain of his future, Elijah reflected on the desires of his childhood and had intimations that his final destiny would be of a religious nature. Recounting a conversation with his mother, he stated:

> I told [her] that it seemed that there was something warning me that I should be a better man, and I should do what I always longed to do since I was a boy and that is to teach a religion or preach ... I [could not] see my way to going to the church telling the preacher that I want to preach the Christian religion as they are preaching. I said something warning me that this is not right.[21]

Elijah Poole was moved in the direction of Fard by his father. The elder Poole recommended that Elijah go to hear the preaching of Abdul Muhammad, a former follower of Noble Drew Ali and new convert to the Nation. [22] Accompanied by his brother, Elijah did so, and was impressed by what he heard. Later, Elijah heard Fard himself speak, and was convinced. At the

---

[19]These three achievements are indicative of the group's final goals. Changing education and the institution of the family, and challenging the state's monopoly of force are the logical first steps in "changing the world."

[20]Hatim A. Sahib, *The Nation of Islam*, p. 90.

[21]*Ibid.*, p. 91.

[22]*Ibid.* Abdul Muhammad later left the group to form a competing organization based on absolute loyalty to the American flag. It was a short-lived venture. C.E. Lincoln, *The Black Muslims in America*, p. 18.

second lecture he attended, he spoke with Fard following the meeting. That moment was of great import in the Nation's development. Elijah recounted:

> when I got to him I shaked my hands with him and told him that I recognized who he is and he held his head down close to my face and he said to me, "Yes, Brother." I said to him: "You are that one we read in the Bible that he would come in the last day under the name Jesus." ... finally he said; "Yes, I am the one that you have been looking for in the last two thousand years ..."[23]

Fard, who had previously not promoted himself as Allah, seemed taken aback by Elijah's declaration. He quickly adopted the role, however, and seized the opportunity presented by the Nation's next meeting to describe himself as "the Jesus" his followers had been waiting for.[24]

During the months following his revelation of Fard's divinity, Elijah attended the Nation's meetings regularly. One evening in the fall of 1931, Elijah stayed home with his children in order that his wife Clara might attend.

> That night he asked about me, saying, "Anyone here in this hall know the little man who lives in Hamtramck?" My wife answered, "Yes he is my husband." ... He told her to tell me to go ahead and teach Islam and he will back me up ... I felt so happy when my wife told me that. I said to myself, "Now, we really have something to teach, and it is good."[25]

He became one of Wallace Fard's most faithful ministers, and was soon given his Muslim name, Elijah Muhammad. Although Muhammad was the third

---

[23]Hatim A. Sahib, *The Nation of Islam*, pp. 91-92.

[24]*Ibid.*, p. 92.

[25]*Ibid.*

minister Fard had chosen, he was the leader's favourite. [26]

Almost from its inception, the Nation attracted controversy. Perhaps the most infamous of their original tenets was a belief that was preached only in the very early years of its history. Wallace Fard taught his followers that the murder of four Whites would insure a free journey to Mecca. This teaching was bound to draw the attention of the police. Although some disagreement regarding this tenet exists within scholarly literature, Elijah Muhammad stated that

> W.D. Fard did teach us that everyone kills four devils at the proper
> time he will have free transportation to Mecca. This teaching had
> stirred the police department in Detroit against him. Ever since,
> they began to persecute us and charge us ... [27]

In his book *Black Nationalism*, Essien-Udom ties this teaching to the Fall of America, noting that some followers claim it is

> ... symbolic, representing the "Four Beasts" in the Book of Reve-
> lation which are said to stand in the way between the destruction
> of the present world and the emergence of the New World.[28]

Although this belief appears to have been temporary, at least one sacrifice was offered. In his article "The Voodoo Cult Among Negro Migrants in Detroit," Erdmann Beynon reports that Robert Karriem sacrificed his roomer, John

---

[26]Hatim A. Sahib, *The Nation of Islam*, p. 96. The first two were Abdul Muhammad and Othman Ali. Both were later accused by Fard of preaching the doctrine of the Moorish Science Temple.

[27]*Ibid.*, p. 95.

[28]E.U. Essien-Udom, *Black Nationalism*, p. 227. Louis Lomax also writes that the teaching "is a matter of record," but does not document his statement. Louis Lomax, *When the Word is Given* ..., (Cleveland: World Publishing Co., 1963), p. 53.

Smith, on November 21, 1932.[29] The following day, two welfare workers were apparently threatened with the same fate.[30]

On May 4, 1933, after his third arrest, Fard was expelled from Detroit by civic authorities;[31] as many legends concern his disappearance as surround his origins. Lincoln notes that critics of Elijah Muhammad point to the coincidence of Fard's disappearance "at the moment of Elijah Muhammad's rise to power."[32] Although he virtually dismisses this idea, Lincoln adds that rumours continue to persist that Muhammad offered Fard as a sacrifice to Allah. Elijah Muhammad himself maintains Fard first moved to Chicago, and then travelled across the United States, returning briefly to Chicago in February of 1934. At any rate, Fard's last contact with Elijah was a letter from Mexico.[33] Marsh notes his "absence fortified the belief that he was God momentarily assuming a human form . . ."[34]

Many groups attempted to take advantage of the Nation's instability at this time to infiltrate and win its followers. Among them were the American Communist Party, [35] the Japanese (under Major Takahashi), and an Ethiopian, (Wyxzewizard S.E. Challouehliczilczese).[36] None was successful, but their combined effect weakened the movement.

---

[29]Erdmann D. Beynon, "The Voodoo Cult Among Negro Migrants in Detroit," *American Journal of Sociology*, May 1938, 43, p. 904.

[30]C. Eric Lincoln, "Extremist Attitudes in the Black Muslim Movement," *Journal of Social Issues*, 19, April 1963, p. 78. Lincoln adds that it is not surprising that welfare workers were accorded this type of sentiment. They were often considered "symbolic of the white man's amorality." *Ibid.*

[31]Louis Lomax, *When the Word is Given* . . ., p. 70.

[32]C.E. Lincoln, *The Black Muslims in America*, p. 17.

[33]Hatim A. Sahib, *The Nation of Islam*, p. 71.

[34]C. Marsh, *From Black Muslims to Muslims*, p. 54.

[35]C. E. Lincoln, *The Black Muslims in America*, p. 18.

[36]E. D. Beynon, "The Voodoo Cult Among Negro Migrants in Detroit," p. 904.

Fard's disappearance was a blow to the group; factionalism already present was exaggerated by loss of the group's divine inspiration. In particular, conflict between Elijah Muhammad and his younger brother threatened the stability of the movement. Elijah recounted:

> In the fall of 1934 most of the followers turned out to be hypocrites and they began to teach against the movement, and to join the enemies of the movement. The situation got so bad that in 1935 it was impossible to go among them because it seemed to me that over 75 per cent of them were hypocrites. And therefore I had to leave them to save my own life. Hypocrisy was arising even within my house; my youngest brother, who was living in my house with another assistant minister, aligned against me because he wanted the teachings for himself. They joined my enemy here and in Detroit and they began to seek my life. So Allah warned me to leave.[37]

As a consequence of this perceived danger, Elijah Muhammad left Detroit, and for a period of seven years remained in hiding. Sahib notes that this time was not wasted. Muhammad continued to preach, perhaps spurred on by the vision of an imminent millennium. Elijah claimed that during this period the voice of Wallace Fard directed his actions.[38] He apparently travelled across the United States, but spent most of these years preaching in Washington D.C. under the name Mohammad Rasool.[39]

In early 1942, Elijah established the headquarters of the Nation of Islam in Chicago. Although the movement had attained a membership of over eight thousand in Detroit, the many years of internal fighting had diminished its

---

[37]Hatim A. Sahib, *The Nation of Islam*, p. 80.

[38]*Ibid.*, p. 97.

[39]*Ibid.*, p. 80.

numbers considerably.[40] Initially, this rebuilding was difficult; in 1942, over one hundred members were arrested for failure to comply with their draft notices.[41] As well, the group could not find a permanent meeting place. These problems were the first of many experiences the Nation was to have with the United States Federal Bureau of Investigation. Elijah Muhammad stated:

> ... we were moving from temple to temple and from district to district just because we did not own our own temple. The white people and the Christian dark people were stimulating the owner of any place we had rented as a temple to compel us to vacate the place through the enforcement agency. The F.B.I. did that many times, telling the landlord to drive us out of his property. This continuous persecution led me to think of buying our own temple.[42]

In 1942, he too was obliged to serve time in prison. Along with eleven other Black leaders, Elijah was arrested by the F.B.I. for preaching sedition[43] and avoiding the draft.[44] His wife Clara played perhaps her most important role in the history of the movement at this time, directing the group's development as it became formally established in Chicago.

With the end of the Second World War, and Elijah's release from prison, the Nation of Islam underwent a period of growth. After purchasing their first Chicago Temple, the group became truly established. The dissemination of their doctrine then began in earnest.

As has been noted, the appeal of the Nation's belief system is in part due to its comprehensive nature. Not only does it provide Blacks with a history

---

[40]C.E. Lincoln, *The Black Muslims in America*, p. 18.

[41]Elijah Muhammad, *The Message to the Blackman in America*, p. 322.

[42]*Ibid.*, p. 87.

[43]C.E. Lincoln, *The Black Muslims in America*, p. 207.

[44]Elijah Muhammad, *The Message to the Blackman in America*, p. 179.

that encompasses the origin of mankind, but it gives meaning to that history. Their doctrine is for the most part contained in three works, the most popular of which is *The Message to the Blackman in America*. Both *The Supreme Wisdom: Solution to the So-Called Negroes' Problem*, and *The Teaching for the Lost Found Nation of Islam in a Mathematical Way* are relatively obscure works. The former document was an early publication of the group that has undergone several revisions,[45] while the latter tract has much the same format as the Christian catechism, and is usually transmitted orally. Access to these documents is difficult, if not impossible, to obtain.[46]

Not surprisingly, the Muslims' original doctrine reflects the religious knowledge and experience of the group. Although they purport to shun Christianity, many of their teachings are strongly linked to the Bible. Biblical myths are repeated with minor changes, and its books used as references for various prophecies. While traditional Islam links the Old and New Testaments with the Qur'an, the heavy emphasis the Nation places on the Christian documents is in part a consequence of the background of Fard, Elijah Muhammad, and their early followers. All were more familiar with the Bible than the Qur'an. The doctrine of the Nation of Islam has changed drastically since the early years of its existence. Outlined below is the original belief system, as presented by Wallace Fard and refined by Elijah Muhammad.

A fundamental tenet of the Nation's doctrine was the belief that God or Allah is not, as Christianity teaches, a spiritual being. The concept of a spir-

---

[45]C.E. Lincoln, *The Black Muslims in America*, p. 139.

[46]Sahib notes that access to *The Teaching for the Lost Found Nation of Islam in a Mathematical Way* is forbidden Whites. Fard warned Elijah Muhammad against allowing this. Included in Sahib's thesis, however, are several excerpts from the work. Hatim A. Sahib, *The Nation of Islam*, p. 148. A copy of *The Supreme Wisdom* is apparently held in the C.E. Lincoln Archives at the Robert Woodsworth Library, Atlanta University Centre, Atlanta, Georgia.

itual deity "enslaves the minds of the ignorant"[47] with the promise of a spiritual hereafter. Allah is a living being whose promises are as material as his
presence on earth in the person of Wallace Fard.[48] While traditional Islam
maintains that the last Prophet of Allah was Muhammad, the Nation of Islam
interpreted Elijah Muhammad as the last Messenger of Wallace Fard. The
Muslims believed the purpose of Fard's visit to have been the awakening of
Black Americans to their status as the Chosen People of Allah; the suffering
they endured in the United States therefore had meaning.

The evil behaviour of Whites was explained by the myth of Yakub. The
Muslims contended that Blacks were the planet's original inhabitants; they
"came with the earth ... 60 trillion years ago."[49] All belonged to the tribe of
Shabazz, which in prehistory lived on an enormous planet. When an explosion
divided that planet into the earth and moon, the tribe of Shabazz survived and
came to inhabit the Nile Valley, one of the most plentiful areas on the earth.
There they lived in harmony for many years.

The serenity of the tribe's civilization at Mecca was disrupted 6,600 years
ago with the birth of Yakub, a boy destined to "break peace, kill and destroy
his own people with a made enemy."[50] While playing with steel, Yakub was
said to have discovered the principle that unlike attracts and like repels; this
idea he transferred to the social realm, determining that to have absolute power
over his people, he would have to create an "unlike man." When later he had
graduated from university, he set about convincing the population of Mecca of

---

[47]Elijah Muhammad, *The Message to the Blackman in America*, p. 3.

[48]The name Fard, which Allah has taken in this, his final journey to earth, is symbolic of
the time at hand. Fard used the term to refer to the first part of the Muslims' morning prayer,
and to symbolize the early morning of the millennium. Elijah Muhammad, *The Message to
the Blackman in America*, p. 141.

[49]Elijah Muhammad, *The Message to the Blackman in America*, p. 31.

[50]*Ibid.*, p. 112. Yakub and his role in Black history are said to have been predicted 8,400
years prior to his birth.

his ideas. Eventually, Yakub and his followers were deported to the island of Pelan. [51]

Once settled, Yakub began to conduct experiments to genetically transform the Black population of the isle into Whites. When this was accomplished he would have found a means by which to enslave the population of Mecca. Over a period of six hundred years, Yakub and his scientists bred out the dark colour of his followers' skin. Elijah Muhammad has stated of Yakub:

> His aim was to kill and destroy the black nation. He ordered the nurses to kill all black babies that were born among his people, by pricking the brains with a sharp needle as soon as the black child's head is out of its mother.[52]

The White population travelled to Mecca when Yakub's experiments were successfully concluded; created out of lies and greed, they were a truly evil people:

> As they [grew] lighter and lighter they grew weaker and weaker. Their blood became weaker, their bones became weaker, their minds became weaker, their morals became weaker.[53]

Not surprisingly, they caused disruption wherever they went and subsequently were banished to Europe.

The Whites lived in Europe as savages for two thousand years, at which

---

[51]Elijah Muhammad, *The Message to the Blackman in America*, pp. 113-14. Elijah Muhammad maintained that the isle of Pelan was that of Patmos, the site of John's revelation of the apocalypse, therefore the "John" of the New Testament was actually Yakub. Malcolm X., "Black Man's History," *The End of White World Supremacy*, Imam Benjamin Karim, (Ed.), (New York: Seaver Books, 1971), p. 53.

[52]*Ibid.*, p. 115

[53]Malcolm X, "Black Man's History," p. 56.

point Allah sent Moses to bring them into civilization.[54] Although the prophet tried to save the Whites, he found this feat to be impossible:

> Once they gave Moses so much trouble that he took a few sticks of dynamite, went up on the mountainside, placed them into the ground, and went back to get [the Whites] who were giving him the most trouble.

> He said to them: "stand there on the edge of this mountainside and you will hear the voice of God." They stood there, about 300 in number. Moses set the fuse off and it killed all of them.[55]

The White devils continued to procreate, however, and soon spread across the globe. Their intrinsically evil nature led them to instigate numerous heinous crimes, the worst of which was the taking of Blacks into slavery. According to Elijah's prophecy, their six thousand year rule of the world was coming to an end. Its demise began in 1914, and was marked by the first World War.[56]

Before the White race could be overthrown, however, Blacks had to come to a knowledge of self. That is, they had to become aware of their history and destiny. Elijah Muhammad referred to this process as the "Resurrection" of Black Americans.[57] His mission would bring about a new life for his people. The history of the tribe of Shabazz, as outlined above, was a crucial motivator. Once Blacks were aware that originally they had the most civilized and perfect society in the world, the possibility of its recurrence would not seem unreasonable. This new version of history filled a large void in the history of

---

[54]Elijah Muhammad notes that "EU stands for hills and cavesides of that continent and ROPE means a place where that people were bound in." Elijah Muhammad, *Message to the Blackman in America*, p. 267.

[55]*Ibid.*, p. 120.

[56]*Ibid.*, p. 142.

[57]*Ibid.*, p. 278.

the Black race, and gave individuals a sense of pride where before there existed only dishonour.

The Muslims' vision of an earthly millennium prompted their strict moral code; its tenets were followed in order that the Nation could return to its previous perfect state. As well, Muslims followed a number of rituals connected with prayer, most of which involved the cleansing of the body. This desire for cleanliness was extended to include internal cleanliness as well; members adhered to strict dietary regulations. Specifically, Elijah Muhammad forbade consumption of the traditional foods of southern Blacks, which he termed a "slave diet."[58] Foods such as cornbread, black-eyed peas, and chitlins were to be avoided. These foods, he maintained, were very hard on the digestive system.[59] Like traditional Muslims, members of the Nation were also prohibited from eating pork. Religious beliefs were the primary basis for this regulation, but the Muslims' venomous warnings concerning its consumption carry hints of the group's more political beliefs:

> The hog is dirty, brutal, quarrelsome, greedy, ugly, foul, a scavenger which thrives on filth. It is a parasite to all other animals. It will even kill and eat its own young ... In short, the hog has all the characteristics of a white man![60]

Elijah also encouraged moderation in eating, asking his followers to consume only one meal each day.[61] Members of the Nation were forbidden to smoke, drink alcohol, take drugs, and gamble.[62]

---

[58] C.E. Lincoln, *The Black Muslims in America*, p. 83.

[59] *Muhammad Speaks*, February 18, 1966, p. 11.

[60] *Ibid.*

[61] *Muhammad Speaks*, February 18, 1966, p. 11.

[62] These tenets of their doctrine are a major factor in members' typical ascending of the

The Muslim leadership also encouraged endogamy. Although divorce was permitted, it was frowned upon. Members were severely punished for such sins as adultery, often being temporarily expelled. The institution of the family was thus emphasized. Lincoln writes,

> Men are expected to live soberly and with dignity, to work hard, to devote themselves to their families' welfare, and to deal fairly with all men ... Modesty, thrift, and service are recommended as [women's] chief concerns. [63]

Interracial marriages were forbidden, and Muslim men were constantly reminded to protect Black women.[64]

As in many groups who believe themselves the Chosen People, Muslim women and children were exalted for their role in continuing the race. Two of the Nation's priorities were thus training women to be good wives and mothers, and educating youth.[65] This focus on the future of the race also helped to foster the development of a birth control conspiracy theory. Elijah Muhammad wrote:

> America desires to keep us a subjugated people. So she, therefore, wants to stop our birth (as Pharaoh did). The Birth Control Law or Act of today is directed at the so-called Negroes and not at the American whites ... They are seeking to destroy our race through our women.[66]

---

social ladder, and the group's clean-up of the ghettos. Today the Muslim community adheres to those tenets practiced by Orthodox Islam.

[63]C.E. Lincoln, *The Black Muslims in America*, p. 86.

[64]Elijah Muhammad, *The Message to the Blackman in America*, p. 58.

[65]As noted above, two of the group's first branch organizations were the Muslim Girls Training Class and the University of Islam.

[66]Elijah Muhammad, *The Message to the Blackman in America*, pp. 66-67. This conspiracy is given much attention in the Nation's publication, *Muhammad Speaks*.

Closely tied to the Muslims' emphasis on knowledge of self and separation of the races was Elijah Muhammad's encouragement of Black self-sufficiency in the economic sphere. Indeed, economic success would emerge naturally from proper Islamic behaviour. Elijah Muhammad offerred the following "blueprint":

(1) Recognize the necessity for unity and group operation (activities). (2) Pool your resources, physically as well as financially. (3) Stop wanton criticisms of everything that is black-owned and black-operated. (4) Keep in mind – jealousy destroys from within. (5) Observe the operations of the white man. He is successful ... [67]

While not specifically part of their religious doctrine, economic self-sufficiency was implicitly tied to the Muslims' religious faith. As will be discussed below, the Nation achieved notable success in many of its economic ventures. While this facet of their belief system eventually saw them become more completely integrated with White society, it was a cornerstone of their demand for complete separation. Economic self-sufficiency was necessary preparation for the acquisition of a separate state and for the arrival of the millennium.

One of the Muslims' most political demands was their desire for a separate state on the North American continent. They wanted not only a biological separation from Whites, but also a physical isolation. In Elijah Muhammad's manifesto "What the Muslims Want," this demand is presented as partial reparation for the years Blacks spent in slavery. He wrote:

We believe that our former slave-masters are obligated to maintain and supply our needs in this separate territory for the next 20 to 25 years until we are able to produce and supply our own needs.[68]

---

[67] Elijah Muhammad, *The Message to the Blackman in America*, p. 174.

[68] *Ibid.* p. 161.

The quantity of land the Muslims requested was usually three or four states, but this amount varied. Lincoln therefore reasoned there are "indications that Muhammad does not really consider the physical separation of the races in [the United States] a viable issue."[69] Two facts indicated that this was a possibility. Elijah Muhammad did not concern himself with concrete plans for this separation, and the Nation's economic holdings are scattered across the United States.[70] Lincoln concluded that this would seem to indicate that the Muslims are prepared to continue tolerating Whites. It is likely, however, that this demand was perceived by the movement as a temporary one, as was the problem of tolerating Whites. In much of the Nation's literature, the demand for land is presented as the last opportunity for White America to redeem itself. The Muslims saw little hope of that occurring. Elijah stated:

> I am not begging for states. It is immaterial to me, if the white government of America does not want to give us anything, just let us go ... Our God will make a way for us.[71]

The impending Fall of America made this demand relatively trivial. If the millennium was imminent, Blacks would soon receive what was truly due to them.

The Muslims' belief in the Fall of America was the logical culmination of their doctrine. For the Nation, the ultimate downfall of Yakub's devils was prophesied in the book of Revelation, and the means by which it was achieved was discussed in Ezekiel. Its occurrence would reintroduce the period of perfect happiness enjoyed by the tribe of Shabazz in Mecca.

Elijah Muhammad noted that it was Wallace Fard who originally predicted

---

[69]C.E. Lincoln, *The Black Muslims in America*, pp. 100-102.

[70]*Ibid.*

[71]Elijah Muhammad, *Muhammad Speaks*, March 13, 1964, p. 4.

the Black millennium.[72] Its expansion and ties to Biblical prophecies appear to have been woven by Elijah himself, however. In *The Message to the Blackman in America*, he explained that the beast described in the book of Revelation was the white race. Blacks "worshiped the dragon who gave power into the beast."[73] The Messenger here made one of his few specific remarks regarding Christianity, noting that it was the Pope of Rome who was the "chief head and spiritual guidance" of the white race.[74]

While all Blacks were susceptible to the devil's wiles, it was women who were his easiest target. The serpent who was able to tempt Eve in the Book of Genesis reappears in Revelation to tempt women again:

> It is his first and last trick to deceive the people of God through the woman or with the woman. He is using his woman to tempt the black man. He stands before the so-called Negro woman to deceive her by feigning love and love-making with her.[75]

The woman referred to in Revelation 12:4 was the last Apostle of God, Elijah Muhammad, and her child was symbolic of the entire Black race who were "not yet ready to be delivered (go to their own)."[76]

The Fall of America had already begun, but few were aware of its development. The demise of the White race was ushered in by World War I, the War of the Anti-Christs,[77] and after a fifty-year period of grace, it was entering its final stages.

---

[72]Elijah Muhammad, *The Message to the Blackman in America*, p. 17.

[73]*Ibid.*, pp. 125-26.

[74]*Ibid.*, p. 126.

[75]*Ibid.*, p. 127. To these comments, Elijah added the note that women were converted to the Nation less frequently than men, (the ratio was five men to one woman in some cities).

[76]*Ibid.*

[77]*Ibid.*, p. 289.

The only reason God didn't remove them then was because [we] were here in their clutches ... they received an extension of time to give the wise men of the East the opportunity to get into this House of Bondage and "awaken" the Lost Sheep.[78]

Because White Americans were the most evil members of their race, the fall of their nation was to occur first.[79] Its demise would stand as a warning to Europe.

For Elijah Muhammad, signs that the Fall was imminent were plentiful in the early 1960s. Indeed, he marked 1965 and 1966 as the years White rule would end.[80] The early 1960s were, in general, a time of social upheaval in the United States. Elijah Muhammad found particular signs important, among them the decline of the American dollar, the threat of "atomic war," and the drought in Kansas and Texas. [81] For the Nation of Islam, the end of America was imminent. As Elijah wrote,

... if there are signs that will be produced before that particular destruction of the old world, how many signs do you know of today that have not been fulfilled that must now be fulfilled? If you know one sign that the Bible refers to that has not yet taken place, point it out to me.[82]

The mechanism that was to usher in the Fall of America was prophesied by Ezekiel. An apocalyptic "battle in the sky" would take place, in which Allah's

---

[78]Malcolm X, "The Black Man's History," p. 65.

[79]*Ibid.*, p. 269. Germans were also marked by Elijah Muhammad as particularly evil.

[80]Elijah made clear that the Qur'anic "Days of Allah" referred to a period of years, not the literal "days."

[81]Elijah Muhammad, *The Message to the Blackman in America*, p. 275.

[82]*Ibid.*, p. 16.

powerful Mother of Planes would fight White America. The Mother of Planes is

> ... one half mile by a half mile and is the largest mechanical man-
> made object in the sky. It is a small human planet made for the pur-
> pose of destroying the present world of the enemies of Allah ... It
> [carries] fifteen hundred bombing planes with the most deadliest
> explosives ... [83]

Evidence of the plane's existence could be found in sightings of flying saucers.

The new age following the battle would be one of perfect peace and happiness. The destruction of unrighteousness would create a heaven on earth:

> No sickness, no hospitals, no insane asylums, no gambling, no curs-
> ing, or swearing will be seen or heard ... Fear, grief and sorrow will
> stop ... [those who follow Allah] will be clothed in silk interwoven
> with gold and eat the best of food ... [84]

After years of pain and suffering at the hands of their oppressors, Black Americans would rise to their rightful position in a perfect world.

Like all millenarian doctrines, the Muslims' belief system held a powerful
attraction for the poor and oppressed. Their strict moral code and emphasis on
self-sufficiency, however, over time transformed the nature of the movement's
membership. With the unintentional assumption of a very middle class way
of life, the Muslims helped to ensure their continued existence after the Fall of
America failed to occur.

---

[83] Malcolm X, "The Black Man's History," p. 29.

[84] Elijah Muhammad, *The Message to the Blackman in America*, p. 304.

Chapter 3

THE FALL OF AMERICA

[W]hen a man understands who he is, who God is, who the devil is ... then he can pick himself up out of the gutter; he can clean himself up and stand up like a man should before his God.[1]

Malcolm X

The middle years of the Nation of Islam's history were perhaps its most eventful; the movement underwent both growth and schism while preparing for the Fall of America. Ultimately, of course, the millennium failed to arrive. This disappointment caused little disruption within the group's membership, however, for in many ways the Muslims had been prepared for this eventuality.

During the late 1940s, the Nation attracted perhaps its most famous convert: Malcolm Little. In background and character, he was typical of many of the Nation's membership. The son of a Baptist preacher and Garveyite, Malcolm learned while young to hate Whites and the American government. His father was killed in 1931 by the Black Legion, and within five years state social workers had split up the Little family. Malcolm drifted into a life of

---

[1]Malcolm X, "A Summing Up: Louis Lomax Interviews Malcolm X," *When the Word is Given* ..., (Cleveland: World Publishing Company, 1963, pp. 197-198.

crime, playing the numbers, bootlegging, stealing, pimping, and selling drugs.[2] At the time he joined the Nation of Islam, Malcolm was serving a seven-year term at the Norfolk Prison colony.

Despite his criminal behaviour, it should be noted that Malcolm was both intelligent and ambitious. While in prison he not only studied grammar and Latin, but each day copied and memorized a page of the dictionary.[3] In 1947, converted by his brother Reginald, he became a member of the Nation of Islam.[4] His new religion became the outlet for his tremendous energy and drive.

Like all converts, Malcolm was required to copy and submit the following letter to Elijah Muhammad:

> Dear Saviour Allah, Our Deliverer,
>
> I have been attending the teachings of Islam by one of your Ministers, two or three times. I believe in It, and I bear witness that there is no God but Thee, and that Muhammad is Thy Servant and Apostle. I desire to reclaim my Own. Please give me my Original Name. My slave name is as follows: ——[5]

This letter, a test of commitment to the Nation, allowed the convert to drop his "slave name" and receive his "Original Name" from Elijah. During the period Malcolm joined the movement, this name was most often an "X," a surname interpreted as having several meanings: it symbolized not only the fact that that the believer was "ex-" what he was prior to conversion, and that

---

[2]Malcolm X with Alex Haley, *The Autobiography of Malcolm X*, (New York: Ballantine Books, 1964), pp. 1-126.

[3]*Ibid.*, pp. 154-57.

[4]C.E. Lincoln, *The Black Muslims in America*, (Boston: Beacon Press, 1973), p. 209.

[5]*Ibid.*, p. 114.

the potentiality and nature of the Muslims were mysterious, but also the fact that Blacks could not know their real names.[6] The importance of this name change was well summarized by James Baldwin:

> It is a fact that every American Negro bears a name that originally belonged to the white man whose chattel he was ... they are both visibly and legally the descendants of slaves in white, Protestant country, and this is what it means to be an American Negro ... [7]

Conversion to the Nation of Islam gave Blacks a new identity.

After leaving prison, Malcolm X became a Muslim recruiter in Detroit;[8] later he was sent to New York to open the first Nation of Islam Temple in Harlem.[9] From the beginning, and perhaps unintentionally, he exerted a great deal of influence upon the affairs of the Nation.

During the 1950s, the organization's growth was rapid, and many attributed its rising membership to his fervent proselytizing. Travelling across the United States many times each year, he was responsible for establishing many of the Nation's Temples. Marsh notes that the individuals Malcolm attracted differed considerably from those converted earlier in the movement's history. This subtle alteration in membership was clearly evidenced in the organization's leadership. Of the nine active ministers in the late 1950s, four had been members prior to 1953. These men had worked long and hard to attain their position; three had joined during the early 1940s and endured jail terms for their beliefs.[10] The five remaining ministers, like Malcolm himself, rose rapidly in

---

[6]Imam B. Karim, "Introduction," *The End of White World Supremacy*, (New York: Seaver Books, 1971), p. 9.

[7]James Baldwin, *The Fire Next Time*, (New York: Dell Publishing, 1962), p. 114.

[8]Malcolm X with Alex Haley, *The Autobiography of Malcolm X*, p. 195.

[9]*Ibid.*, p. 215.

[10]Each had refused to register for the draft.

the Nation's hierarchy and all had at least a high school education.[11] This transformation of leadership is interesting in itself, but becomes especially important when considered in terms of the Nation's development at that time. Marsh writes that it was the late 1950s which saw the Nation's business enterprises begin to flourish.[12] The movement's interaction with White society was increasing, and it was becoming more an established institution than a transitory fringe group. While these changes played no immediate role in the group's activities, they marked the beginning of an important trend.

In 1959, the Nation came to the attention of the American news media. Prompted by Louis Lomax, a Black journalist, Elijah Muhammad consented to the making of a documentary focusing on the movement.[13] Although the Muslims had envisioned the program as a means of proselytizing, this was not to be the case. Entitled "The Hate that Hate Produced," the Mike Wallace documentary was primarily intended to shock its audience. Malcolm X wrote of the incident:

> In a way, the public reaction was like what happened back in the
> 1930s when Orson Welles frightened America with a radio program
> describing ... an invasion by "men from Mars".[14]

Americans were horrified at what they saw, and the mainstream press immediately developed a consuming interest in a group they had previously ignored. This increased attention came at a time when Elijah Muhammad's health was noticeably fading. Indeed, for reasons of health the Messenger was living in Phoenix, Arizona, when the uproar over "The Hate that Hate Produced"

---

[11]C. Marsh, *From Black Muslims to Muslims*, (Metuchen: Scarecrow Press, Inc., 1984), p. 73.

[12]*Ibid.*, p. 74.

[13]Malcolm X with Alex Haley, *The Autobiography of Malcolm X*, p. 236.

[14]*Ibid.*, p. 238.

occurred. As the movement's National Spokesman, Malcolm X became the centre of publicity. To many this increased attention appeared to challenge Elijah Muhammad's leadership. Malcolm swore complete loyalty to Elijah, however, stating,

> ... it's heresy to imply that I am in any way whatever equal to Mr. Muhammad. No man on earth today is his equal. Whatever I am that is good, it is through what I have been taught by Mr. Muhammad.[15]

Nevertheless, it was at this time that a rift seemed to develop between the Messenger and Malcolm. By his distance from the movement's headquarters in Chicago, Elijah had unintentionally created three centres of authority: himself, Malcolm X, and the Chicago bureaucracy. As divine Messenger, his own position was unchallenged. Malcolm however, was left in unintended and certainly unwanted competition with individuals at the group's headquarters. It seems plausible, as Malcolm himself suggests, that the Nation's bureaucracy, like all such institutions, could not help but pursue its own interests.[16]

Despite these problems, it was at this point that the Muslims began publishing their own newspaper. In 1959, one issue of the *Islamic News* appeared, accompanied by the journal *Salaam*; in 1961, a single issue of *The Messenger* was published.[17] These short-lived journals were replaced in 1961 by *Muhammad Speaks*, a newspaper which, at the peak of its success, had a circulation of 600,000, the largest of all Black newspapers in the United States.[18] Mal-

---

[15] Alex Haley, "Malcolm X," *The Playboy Interview*, G. Golson, (Ed.), (U.S.A.: Worldview Books, 1981), p. 49.

[16] Malcolm X with Alex Haley, *The Autobiography of Malcolm X*, p. 290.

[17] Roland Wolseley, *The Black Press, U.S.A.*, (Ames, Iowa: Iowa State University Press, 1971), p. 82.

[18] *Ibid.*, p. 12.

colm X originally published the paper, which featured articles concerning the movement's doctrine and beliefs, and usually included at least one piece by the Messenger himself. Stories concerning the Nation's activities and information regarding international events were also published. In *The Black Press, U.S.A.*, Wolseley characterizes its publishing policy as pro-Arab, anti-Israel, and against American participation in Vietnam.[19] Like most of the Muslims' businesses, *Muhammad Speaks* became a training ground for many Blacks, providing them with skills useful outside the Nation's realm.

In its early years, *Muhammad Speaks* was primarily concerned with doctrinal issues, but the political stance of the Nation can also be traced through its pages. Malcolm X originally figured prominently in the paper. His coverage, however, decreased rapidly between 1961 and 1963. Herbert, Elijah Muhammad's son and the Editor of *Muhammad Speaks* at that time, had apparently instructed that as little as possible be published regarding Malcolm.[20] This decreasing coverage was in part the result of the "rivalry" discussed above, and in part a consequence of the Minister's own behaviour. As 1963 approached, Malcolm made a discovery that tempered his enthusiasm for the Nation, and made him more cautious in his public statements.

Like all Muslims, Malcolm had believed Elijah Muhammad to be "a symbol of moral, mental, and spiritual reform," an example for all Blacks.[21] On July 3, 1963, however, two paternity suits were brought against the Messenger by his former secretaries.[22] For Elijah Muhammad, the divine Messenger of Allah, to have committed such acts was unthinkable. Adultery was considered one of

---

[19]Roland Wolseley, *The Black Press, U.S.A.*, p. 83.

[20]Malcolm X with Alex Haley, *The Autobiography of Malcolm X*, p. 292.

[21]*Ibid.*, p. 294.

[22]In total, Elijah Muhammad fathered fifteen children by his private secretaries. *The Chicago Tribune*, July 11, 1986, p. 1.

the most serious moral offences a Muslim could commit; as noted above, the guilty often faced temporary expulsion. The shock this caused Malcolm was great. He wrote, "... my faith had been shaken in a way that I can never fully describe ... [we] had been betrayed by Elijah Muhammad himself." [23] Assumption of the Messenger's divinity was so closely integrated with the Muslims' religious faith that evidence tending to cast doubt upon it was bound to challenge the entire system of belief.

Malcolm approached Elijah Muhammad himself for an explanation of his leader's behaviour. The Messenger explained his transgressions as the fulfillment of prophecy, saying to Malcolm:

> I'm David ... When you read about how David took another man's wife, I'm that David. You read about Noah who got drunk – that's me. You read about Lot, who went and laid up with his own daughters. I have to fulfill all of these things. [24]

Malcolm accepted his leader's justification, and anticipating the reaction of the press, warned several ministers of the facts. Unfortunately, this backfired; the bureaucracy at Chicago used it as an example of Malcolm's treacherous behaviour. The rift between Malcolm and Elijah thus continued to grow.

On November 22, 1963, John F. Kennedy was assassinated; aware that the President had been much admired by many of his followers, Elijah Muhammad instructed his ministers to make no comment on his murder. [25]

The first speech Malcolm made following the event concerned the imminent Fall of America, and illustrated the Minister's vehement belief in the

---

[23] Malcolm X with Alex Haley, *The Autobiography of Malcolm X*, p. 294.

[24] *Ibid.*, p. 299.

[25] *Ibid.*, p. 300.

apocalypse.[26] He stated:

> You and I are living in that great Doomsday, the final hour, when
> the ancient prophets predicted that God himself would appear in
> person, in the flesh, and with divine power. He would bring about
> the judgment and destruction of this present evil world.[27]

The ruins of White civilization would produce "a world of universal brotherhood that will be based upon the principles of truth, freedom, justice, equality,
righteousness, and peace." [28] Following the Messenger's instructions, Malcolm
made no direct comment on President Kennedy's death. He did, however, remark on what he perceived to be the late President's manipulation of Blacks,
inferring that Kennedy's assassination was only to be expected.[29]

During the question and answer period that followed his speech, this line of
thought prompted Malcolm to make a remark that directly contravened Elijah
Muhammad's orders. It terminated his career with the Nation of Islam. When
asked for his opinion on Kennedy's assassination, he characterized it as

> ... chickens [coming] home to roost ... being an old farm boy
> myself, chickens coming home to roost never did make me sad;
> they've always made me glad.[30]

This injudicious remark provided the ideal opportunity for the Nation to silence
him. Malcolm was forbidden to speak to the press and perform his ministerial
functions for a period of ninety days, a chastisement only briefly noted in

---

[26]Malcolm X, "God's Judgement of America," *The End of White World Supremacy*, pp.
121-48.

[27] *Ibid.*, p. 124.

[28] *Ibid.*

[29] *Ibid.*, pp. 139-40.

[30] *The New York Times*, December 2, 1963, p. 21

Muhammad Speaks.[31] Malcolm accepted his punishment with little complaint, and went to Florida for a holiday; there he converted Cassius Clay to the Nation of Islam.

During Malcolm's ninety-day silencing, he spoke often with Elijah Muhammad. The rift between the two men only grew wider, however, and in January of 1964 Malcolm was removed from the position of Minister at Temple 7. That same month, Elijah excommunicated his son Wallace for working too closely with Malcolm.[32]

On March 8, 1964, Malcolm X formally announced his departure from the Nation of Islam.[33] At that time he organized a new religious group, the Muslim Mosque Inc.; later in the the year he founded its political wing, the Organization of Afro-American Unity, (O.A.A.U.). Malcolm was well aware that his actions would disturb many within the ranks of the Nation of Islam. Indeed, his decision to make his pilgrimmage to Mecca (the Hajj), was motivated not only by commitment to his faith, but also out of fear for his life, should he remain in the United States.[34]

The great changes Malcolm underwent during his journey to the Middle East are common knowledge today. While making the Hajj, he talked and prayed with Muslims "whose eyes were the bluest of blue, whose hair was the blondest of blond, and whose skin was the whitest of white."[35] Foreshadowing changes which ten years later were to drastically alter the Nation of Islam, Malcolm wrote of his experience:

---

[31] *Muhammad Speaks*, December 20, 1963, p. 3.

[32] C. Marsh, *From Black Muslims to Muslims*, p. 79. Wallace Muhammad later became a pivotal figure in the movement's history.

[33] *Ibid.*, p. 80.

[34] Malcolm X with Alex Haley, *The Autobiography of Malcolm X*, pp. 316-17.

[35] *Ibid.*, p. 340.

> We were *truly* all the same (brothers) – because their belief in one
> God had removed the 'white' from their *minds*, the 'white' from
> their *behavior*, and the 'white' from their *attitude*.[36]

Malcolm X returned to the United States in June of 1964. Reflecting his conversion to traditional, Orthodox Islam, he changed his name to El Hajj Malik El-Shabazz.[37]

Malcolm's departure caused disruption within the Nation of Islam. In June, Hassan Sharrieff, Elijah's grandson, was expelled for deviating from the Messenger's teachings, and a few months later, a similar fate befell Akbar Muhammad, one of Elijah's sons.[38] (The latter had praised the teachings of Malcolm and Wallace.)

When it became clear that Malcolm was not to return to the Nation's fold, he was attacked vehemently in *Muhammad Speaks*.[39] Philbert X, Malcolm's brother, authored a series of articles which began in April of 1964. All were general condemnations of Malcolm's "hypocrisy":

> Now I see my brother pursue a dangerous course which parallels
> that of the precedents set by Judas, Brutus, Benedict Arnold and
> others who betrayed the feduciary [sic] relationship between them
> and their leaders.[40]

Minister Louis (Farrakhan), later a prominent figure in the movement, explained Malcolm's behaviour in terms of prophecy. He wrote:

---

[36] Malcolm X with Alex Haley, *The Autobiography of Malcolm X*, p. 340.

[37] C. Marsh, *From Black Muslims to Muslims*, p. 82.

[38] *Muhammad Speaks*, January 1, 1965, p. 9.

[39] It is interesting to note that as the departure of Malcolm X became a problem for the group, the number of articles and photographs in *Muhammad Speaks* concerning Muhammad Ali, the Minister's most famous convert, substantially increased.

[40] *Muhammad Speaks*, April 10, 1964, p. 3.

Malcolm is fulfilling the prophetic role of Korah, the wealthy (popular) one who rebelled against the leadership of Moses because he
coveted Moses' position.[41]

These internal difficulties occurred during the period Elijah Muhammad
had marked for the Fall of America. Understandably many believers, as well
as the Nation's leadership, interpreted them as the final evils of the Old World.
Minister Louis accurately summarized the belief and hopes of many when he
wrote that this time was "a great trial of our faith, but also ... the greatest
hour of opportunity."[42] These tribulations were to be the last. The urgency of
the time prompted Elijah Muhammad to make the focus of his 1964 Saviour's
Day address "Our Day is Near at Hand." His *Muhammad Speaks* articles of
that year often concerned America's impending doom, and all closed with the
following warning: "HURRY AND JOIN UNTO YOUR OWN KIND. THE
TIME OF THIS WORLD IS AT HAND."[43]

1965 had been marked by the Muslims as the year of the apocalypse, and it
opened with an event that drew international attention to the Nation. On the
afternoon of February 21, Malik Shabazz was assassinated while addressing a
meeting of his new political movement, the O.A.A.U. Mystery still surrounds
the killing: the murderers' identity remains indefinite, as does their motive.[44]
While many assumed the assassination to be the result of Malik's leaving the
Nation of Islam, (a belief reinforced by the fact that all convicted were followers
of Elijah Muhammad), some writers believe that the F.B.I. played a role in

---

[41]*Muhammad Speaks*, June 5, 1964, p. 8. Minister Louis was somewhat prophetic himself.
Later in the article he equated Malcolm with Cain, noting that after slaying his brother Abel
the latter stated, "Everyone that sees me shall slay me."

[42]*Muhammad Speaks*, July 31, 1964, p. 13.

[43]*Muhammad Speaks*, January 31, 1964, p. 8, for example.

[44]George Breitman *et al.* investigate this question in detail in their book, *The Assassination
of Malcolm X*, (New York: Pathfinder Press, 1976).

its instigation. The government had much to gain from Malik's death, while Elijah Muhammad benefitted little.

Not surprisingly, Malik's assassination received little overt attention from the Nation. *Muhammad Speaks*, for example, carried only a few brief articles related to it; most expressed the general view that "the tragedy of the event [lay] not in the violent nature of Malcolm's death but in the role he had unfortunately chosen to play since his separation from the "Nation of Islam."[45] One day after Malik's assassination the Nation of Islam mosque in Harlem was bombed, and the following afternoon, their San Fransisco building was set on fire.[46]

Anticipation of the Fall of America was growing among the Nation's membership. In 1965 *Muhammad Speaks* published articles concerning it with much greater frequency than in previous years. Its cover stories carried such titles as "Break Up of the Old World," (February 12), "The Final Struggle," (May 14), and "God's Anger Against America," (September 24); Elijah Muhammad's articles almost always concerned the impending apocalypse. The organization's preoccupation with the Fall was, however, best evidenced in the March 19 edition of *Muhammad Speaks*. The centrefold of the paper, usually reserved for Elijah Muhammad's personal messages, was in this issue filled with a giant cartoon depicting the apocalypse. Its artist, E. Majied, wrote:

> This is a true picture; there is no doubt in it. Let us follow him as
> he advises us – for that great day of the Lord has come!" II Peter,
> 3:10 and Rev. 6:17.[47]

Concern regarding America's coming Fall was expressed in other facets of

[45]*Muhammad Speaks*, March 5, 1965, p. 9.

[46]Malcolm X with Alex Haley, *The Autobiography of Malcolm X*, pp. 441-442.

[47]*Muhammad Speaks*, March 19, 1965, pp. 12-13.

the Muslims' doctrine as well. The birth control conspiracy became an important concern and was featured in the July editions of *Muhammad Speaks*. Interestingly, the Muslims now perceived the Catholic Church to be the perpetrator of this plot:

> The Catholic religion is our greatest enemy today. It seeks to woo you into its net where your future will be hopeless in the Hereafter.[48]

Despite the increased urgency with which the millennial prediction was viewed, early 1965 saw a subtle reinterpretation already taking place. For example, in the February 12 edition of *Muhammad Speaks*, Elijah Muhammad wrote:

> The day of decision between the dark races or nations was begun by God Himself in the Person of Master Fard Muhammad ... as is prophesied in the Bible: "Multitudes in the valley of decision, for the day *(before or by 1970)* [emphasis added] of the Lord is near in the valley of decision." Joel 3:16.[49]

The Messenger had begun to prepare for the possibility of his prophecy's failure.

Most Muslims remained convinced, however, that the Fall of America had already begun. The cover format of the July 30 edition of *Muhammad Speaks* differed significantly from its usual design; the first paragraphs of the editorial were featured in large print, under the heading, "We are in the Cross-Fire." The article opened with a clear statement that the process of America's Fall had already begun:

---

[48]*Muhammad Speaks*, July 2, 1965, p. 8.

[49]*Muhammad Speaks*, February 12, 1965, p. 3.

> All signs of the times point to the fact that the day of judgment
> is not some "far-away" day coming in the distant future – but a
> day that has already dawned and that the black man in America
> is caught in its terrible cross-fire.[50]

The turmoil America was involved in outside her borders and the difficulties
she faced within were interpreted as evidence of this fact. Black Americans,
the "Chosen People," were caught in the centre of this disruption:

> ... in the awesome Armageddon that looms, if America is attacked
> or provokes an all-out war, black men and women must remember it
> is they who are in the center ... only the guidance of a modern day
> Moses, the Messenger of Allah, can lead to salvation and security
> and to the new world to come.[51]

For the Nation of Islam, the events of 1965 clearly indicated that the Fall of
America was underway.

The first edition of *Muhammad Speaks* in 1966 reinforced this belief. Its
cover story, "Battle in the Sky," tied the prophecy of Ezekiel's Wheel to the
American space program. The United States was preparing for the final battle.
Elijah Muhammad wrote of White America's plans:

> Having knowledge of what they might expect today, they are spend-
> ing billions of dollars on space travel. He has now brought the moon
> to him and even some of the stars ... The Holy Koran further says
> that whenever God gets ready to destroy a people, He opens up the

---

[50]*Muhammad Speaks*, July 30, 1965, p. 1.

[51]*Ibid.*, p. 10. This editorial also seems to evidence an attempt to reconsolidate the Nation
around Elijah Muhammad, after the turmoil of the previous year.

Heavens for them and gives them the pleasure of what they seek or lust after.[52]

In this same issue, "A Look Back at 1965, Muhammad's Forecasts Startled America," discussed the events of 1965 that illustrated the truth of the Messenger's prophecy:

Many pundits and lesser people were quick to point the finger of derision and scoff at the Messenger of Allah's warning. But as 1965 moves into history, those who jeered early in 1965, now stand sheepish, mute and confounded as they read in the white press that 1965 in America has been indeed A Year of Disaster.[53]

The article listed record levels of traffic deaths, and tornados, hurricanes, and floods as part of the destruction wrought upon the United States by Allah.[54]

April of 1966 saw *Muhammad Speaks* feature a story concerning U.F.O. sightings. For the Muslims the appearance of U.F.O.s was a precursor to the apocalyptic Battle in the Sky, and therefore of great importance. The article noted that, exemplifying Whites' refusal to acknowledge the Fall, the United States Air Force denied any knowledge of their occurrence.[55]

Reinforcing the Muslims's belief in the Fall, Elijah Muhammad's article in that edition of the paper, "The Truth!," was for the most part a statement of the group's more political beliefs. It concluded with the following statement:

It is true ... that this year 1966, of the Christian calendar, and which is 1386 of the Arabic calendar, is the fateful year of America

---

[52]*Muhammad Speaks*, January 7, 1966, pp. 1-2.

[53]*Ibid.*, pp. 5-6.

[54]This same type of article appeared in the May 13, 1966 edition of the paper as well, pp. 26-27.

[55]*Muhammad Speaks*, April 1, 1966, p. 2

and her people, and that the so-called Negroes should fly to Allah and follow Messenger Muhammad for refuge from the dreadful
judgments that Allah has said that He will bring, and which have
already begun upon America. [56]

Clearly the Muslims now viewed the period of 1965-66 as initiating the Fall of
America.

This period of general disruption was marked by an expansion of the Nation's economic holdings and a consolidation of its membership. Aside from
their aim of rebuilding the Harlem mosque, the Muslims were at this time also
planning to buy farms and lease land in the Southwestern United States, in
order to "fight poverty and want among black Americans."[57] As well, they
planned to build a new office building in South Chicago.

The apocalypse failed to occur in 1965 and 1966. Following this, references
to the millennium almost completely disappeared from the Nation's rhetoric
between 1967 and 1969. Little was published concerning the Muslims during
this period, a fact which makes it difficult to gauge the group's immediate
response to the "failure" of Elijah's prophecy. In one of the group's few interviews during this period, however, evidence for two behaviours typical of
disillusioned millenarians can be found. In Minister Louis' words can be seen
the beginning of a changed emphasis in the Muslims' belief system:

The purpose was to give the black pride in himself and love for
himself as the first stage. The second is that he should start to
build for himself – we are in the second stage now.[58]

---

[56] *Muhammad Speaks*, April 1, 1966, p. 2. See Appendix II. Harriet Muhammad later
clarified these dates, noting that the Arabic year 1386 was "roughly the year from April, 1966,
to April, 1967." *Muhammad Speaks*, October 7, 1966, p. 19.

[57] *Muhammad Speaks*, July 1, 1966, p. 1.

[58] *The New York Times*, January 13, 1969, p. 44.

As well, the Nation seemed to have placed an increased emphasis on proselytizing. Captain Joseph X reported that membership had increased three hundred
percent since 1964.[59]

Increasing moderation was fostered not only by the failure of Elijah Muhammad's prophecy and the Nation's rapid economic growth, but also by its many
social programs. Although the Muslims' doctrine advocated a collective salvation, the high moral standards and emphasis on self-sufficiency found in
its tenets encouraged believers to help their non-Muslim neighbors. In these
endeavours, they achieved notable success. James Baldwin wrote of their community work:

> Elijah Muhammad has been able to do what generations of welfare
> workers ... have failed to do: to heal and redeem drunkards and
> junkies, to convert people who have come out of prison, and to keep
> them out, to make men chaste and women virtuous, and to invest
> [them] with a pride and a serenity that hang about them like an
> unfailing light.[60]

In this way, the Muslims became more closely integrated with the larger Black
community. In June of 1969 they accepted an award from the National Society
of Afro-American Policemen for their work in the ghettos of the urban United
States.[61]

Although the movement was relatively stable during the late 1960s, some
conflict concerning the leadership seemed to be developing. There was no

---

[59] *The New York Times*, December 13, 1969, p. 44. This publicized increase in membership may have been an attempt by the Nation to obscure any negative effect that Malcolm's
defection may have caused and promote the image of a united and strong following.

[60] James Baldwin, *The Fire Next Time*, p. 72.

[61] *The New York Times*, June 16, 1969, p. 29. For Elijah Muhammad's remarks concerning
the event see *Muhammad Speaks*, June 27, 1969, p. 4.

challenge to Elijah Muhammad's authority, but among the membership some dissatisfaction apparently existed with those immediately surrounding the Messenger. Elijah's health was failing,[62] and his higher level subordinates were likely assuming more responsibility than ever before. No concrete evidence of a conflict emerged until 1972, but the nature of the dissension at that time makes logical the assumption that it had been developing for a number of years. One of the most effective ways to combat this type of difficulty was to emphasize unity in the context of a millennium.

Greater economic growth was also important to the movement during this period. The Nation had achieved much during its history, but one vision of Elijah Muhammad's remained beyond his grasp: a Black-run hospital on the South Side of Chicago. In 1969 he stepped up his campaign to achieve that dream. Elijah wrote:

Send your checks over to me and help me to buy a hospital for our Black selves. Help me to buy Black banks for your and my money ... If you even offered me $1.00 ... I will thank you because Allah (God) is on our side to build a Black Nation out of one that has fallen so deeply ... Not only is our Black Nation to become the equal, but it is to become the superior of the nations of Earth, as it is written ... [63]

Once again a future of prosperity and happiness served as the motivating force.

Indeed, during 1968, references to the Fall of America reappeared in the Nation's rhetoric. Their occurrence was sporadic, however, and in content

---

[62]During these years, Elijah Muhammad's articles in *Muhammad Speaks* were often reprints of his past publications rather than new work, (see, for example, *Muhammad Speaks*, June 20, 1969). As well, the centrefold of the paper, usually reserved for the Messenger's articles, was taken over by others, (see, for example, *Muhammad Speaks*, August 15, 1969, p. 20). Both of these facts hint at the Messenger's failing health.

[63]*Muhammad Speaks*, October 17, 1969, p. 21.

they were far less specific than the prophecies of the mid-1960s. The prophecy appeared to be undergoing a process of reinterpretation: in these articles it is often difficult to determine if the author of a particular statement believes the apocalypse to be a distinct historical event, or if he sees it as a symbol for the disarray of White society in general. This new way of discussing the eschaton was evident in Elijah Muhammad's 1968 Saviour's Day address. To ten thousand followers the Messenger declared that "... the white man's world is falling to pieces."[64] While he acknowledged that the white regime's "time was up," he mentioned no date for its final demise.[65] The frequency of this type of allusion to the Fall of America gradually increased. By April of 1969, they had begun once more to figure prominently in *Muhammad Speaks.*

Accompanying the many references to the millennium was a renewed emphasis on the birth control conspiracy. In part a response to the Nixon administration's policies regarding abortion and voluntary sterilization, the Muslims' concern was reinforced by their religious beliefs.

Warnings of the apocalypse continued throughout 1970 and 1971. Most evidenced reinterpretation and de-eschatologizing either implicitly or explicitly. In "America Surrounded With the Judgments of Allah," for example, Elijah described the disasters befalling America, but made no mention of the millennium that awaited Blacks,

> The four (4) Great Judgments that Almighty Allah (God) Is Bringing upon America are RAIN, HAIL, SNOW and EARTHQUAKES. We see them now covering all sides of America, as the Holy Quran prophesies of 'curtailing her on all sides'... [66]

---

[64] *New York Times*, February 26, 1968, p. 9.

[65] *Ibid.*

[66] *Muhammad Speaks*, January 9, 1970, p. 16.

Likewise, while Elijah still issued warnings concerning "the times" and the separation of the races, they had lost much of their original urgency. The historical experience of Blacks in America had always been a factor in the Muslims' emphasis on separation of the races, but it had been overshadowed by their expectation of the imminent demise of White civilization. By the 1970s even Elijah Muhammad had begun to emphasize the more concrete factor of experience.[67] A specific example of Elijah Muhammad's de-eschatologizing of the Muslims' millennium appeared in the the February 19, 1971 issue of *Muhammad Speaks.* There he wrote:

> I have the key to your salvation and I have the key to your hell. I
> can, if you will let me, pull you out of hell and set you in heaven.[68]

The Messenger was here clearly speaking in metaphorical terms. The way of life one adopted after conversion to the Nation had become the ideal. The religious community now appeared to represent the millennium. In this new form the Fall of America continued to be an important part of the Nation's doctrine.

In late 1971, the undercurrent of dissension within the Nation became violent, and as *The Chicago Tribune* reported, it seemed "based on the refusal of lieutenants of Muhammad to give younger members a voice or stake in financial policies."[69] On October 21, Raymond Sharrieff, Elijah Muhammad's son-in-law, chief bodyguard, and President of the Nation of Islam Inc., was injured when five bullets were fired at him as he walked near the offices of *Muhammad Speaks.*[70] As apparent retribution for this attack, two members

---

[67]*Muhammad Speaks*, January 23, 1970, pp. 16-17.

[68]*Muhammad Speaks*, February 19, 1971, p. 16.

[69]*The Chicago Tribune*, January 14, 1972, p. 17.

[70]*Ibid.*

of the small dissident group, Donald 7X Veira and Freddie 5X Webb, were later found murdered in their homes.[71] In December, a guard at the Muslims' Salaam Restaurant in Chicago, Theodore Bey, was shot.[72]

This violence continued during 1972. In January, a street battle occurred in Baton Rouge, Louisiana, in which four people were killed. While it was never clear how many of those involved were Muslims, or what their motives may have been, seven of the Blacks arrested were from Chicago.[73] Elijah Muhammad declared that the Nation of Islam had nothing to do with the events in Baton Rouge,[74] but in a later press conference, he stated that he was unsure whether those involved were Muslims.[75]

Elijah Muhammad's January 1972 meeting with members of the press was no doubt intended to still rumours regarding the Nation's internal strife and distance the group from the events at Baton Rouge. It is difficult to determine whether this goal was achieved; the Messenger was far from specific when addressing those issues. The interview did, however, shed light on Elijah Muhammad's perception of the Fall of America at that time, and hinted at his vision of the Nation's future development.[76]

Elijah's remarks at this time were cryptic. Although he gave a detailed description of a violent apocalypse, his discussion of the millennium was relatively moderate. Regarding the future of the White race, Elijah stated,

There will be no such thing as elimination of all white people from

---

[71] *The Chicago Tribune*, January 13, 1972, Sec. 1D, p. 2.

[72] *Ibid.*

[73] *Ibid.*

[74] *Muhammad Speaks*, January 21, 1972, p. 2.

[75] *The Chicago Tribune*, January 15, p. 1.

[76] The mainstream press gave the event only limited coverage. A complete transcript is included, in three installments, in *Muhammad Speaks*, (January 28, 1972, pp. 3-4., February 4, 1972, pp. 3-4, and February 11, 1972, pp. 3-4.).

> the earth, at the present time or at the break out of the Holy
> War ... through Islam ... white people can be saved.[77]

The door was thus opened, albeit only slightly, for the Muslims to adopt a more favourable attitude towards Whites. At the same time, however, Elijah warned that a Holy War involving the forces of "wrong" (the Whites), and those of "right," (the Blacks), was inevitable.[78] He added that he did not know what weapons Whites would employ, but that Blacks would achieve victory through God. To a White reporter Elijah stated:

> ... we are not to use carnal weapons ... God Has [sic] every kind of
> weapon there to use against you, even the earth you are sitting on.
> If He Shakes [sic] that for a half a minute, all of your cities could be
> sprawled ... You cannot win in anything ... You cannot stop the
> snow and cold weather from blowing down from the Northwest.[79]

While still vehemently anti-White, he no longer envisioned the demise of White civilization as imminent. Rather, it was to occur at some point after his death. Questioned regarding the future leadership of the Nation (a query obviously tied to the violence of the previous months), Elijah responded that he would have no successor:

> After setting up the nation on the right way, or right path, to
> take care of themselves, they do not need any more instruction on
> that ... the whole entire Nation of Black people will be governed
> divinely ... We will have a Divine government set up for us, and
> it will stand forever.[80]

---

[77] *Muhammad Speaks*, February 11, 1972, p. 4.

[78] *Ibid.*

[79] *Ibid.*

[80] *Muhammad Speaks*, February 4, 1972, p. 4.

Likewise, the Muslims would achieve a position of supremacy in their religion. Elijah stated,

> We have a New Islam coming up. The Old Islam was led by white
> people, white Muslims, but this one will not be. This Islam will be
> established and led by Black Muslims only.[81]

By retaining the fundamental elements of his prophecy, Elijah was able to continue using the Fall of America to consolidate and motivate members of the Nation, despite the postponement of the millennium. Throughout 1972, references to the apocalypse were frequent in his writing.[82] Indeed, during the spring, Elijah Muhammad gave a series of lectures entitled "The Theology of Time."[83] These articles focused on the importance of time in the Nation's doctrine, but were generally vague regarding the date of the millennium's arrival.

In early May, the Nation received a three million dollar loan from the Government of Libya.[84] The first gesture of what was to become an ongoing relationship, the loan provided funds for the Muslims' new Temple in South Chicago, and signified the recognition of their faith by an Islamic country.[85] This acceptance was reinforced later in 1972 when the Prime Minister of Abu Dabhi[86] and Qatar's Minister of Finance[87] visited Elijah Muhammad; both presented the Nation with cheques to further the cause of Islam in the United States. While the declaration that "Widespread financial support of the Lost

---

[81] *Muhammad Speaks*, February 4, 1972, p. 4.

[82] Elijah's *Muhammad Speaks* articles of that year carried such titles as "The Terrible Day of the Lord is Come," (May 12, 1972), "The Cruel Days of the Lord," (May 26, 1972), and "Every Nation Has a Term," (September 15, 1972).

[83] *Muhammad Speaks*, July 7, 1972, pp. S7-S10.

[84] *Muhammad Speaks*, May 19, 1972, pp. 16-17.

[85] *Muhammad Speaks*, June 9, 1972, p. 4.

[86] *Muhammad Speaks*, October 20, 1972, p. 6.

[87] *Muhammad Speaks*, October 27, 1972, p. 4.

Found Nation of Islam is now a reality throughout the Islamic world" [88] was no doubt an exaggeration, the Muslims were clearly becoming more acceptable in the international Islamic community.[89]

In January of 1973, the Muslims purchased the Guaranty Bank and Trust Company of South Chicago as part of their plan to build an independent Black nation,

> As we mature into adulthood as a People, we must recognize and understand the use of "money science." ... We have millions of dollars scattered throughout the country in the Banks and Institutions of the slave-master. Let us show our maturity and Wisdom by pooling our dollars as others have done for the benefit of Self.[90]

Despite its continued expansion, however, hints that the Nation's business empire was in trouble had begun to appear. These rumours were confirmed by a Muslim leader who reported to *The New York Times*:

> Coming from the streets and prisons, we have reached the limit of our ability to manage such a financial empire, and we need the help of professional blacks.[91]

The upper levels of the Nation's bureaucracy denied that a problem existed; it was not until 1976 that the organization's nine million dollar debt was made public.

---

[88]*Muhammad Speaks*, October 27, 1972, p. 4.

[89] *The New York Times* reported that these funds were the result of a direct solicitation made by John Ali (Elijah Muhammad's son) and claimed that the money was given in exchange for a promise that the Nation would move closer towards Orthodox Islam. *The New York Times*, December 6, 1973, p. 37.

[90]*Muhammad Speaks*, January 19, 1973, p. 2.

[91] *The New York Times*, December 6, 1973, p. 37.

Throughout this period, internal strife continued to plague the Nation. During 1972, articles concerning "traitors and deserters," and "the haters of Muhammad" could be found in *Muhammad Speaks*.[92] In May, Hakim Jamal was shot,[93] and in early September, James Shabazz, Minister of the Newark Temple, was murdered.[94] As well, *The Chicago Tribune* reported that since Donald 7X Veira's death in 1971, three other members of his dissident group had been murdered in San Fransisco.[95] This violence, although severe, did not seem to leave a lasting mark on the Nation. After reaching a peak in late 1973, the murders came to a halt.

One of the most important issues for the Muslims today is the degree to which Elijah Muhammad tempered his hatred of Whites and moved closer to Orthodox Islam during the last years of his life. The documentary record of this period is insufficient to draw an unqualified conclusion regarding this question. Nevertheless, evidence exists for two dissimilar but not contradictory observations. Elijah's 1970-75 articles, interviews, and speeches indicate that he continued to identify Whites with the forces of evil and to envision a Black millennium. At the same time, however, he seemed to be moving closer to traditional Islam. Not only did he tone down his anti-White rhetoric, but his vision of the Fall of America was de-eschatologized.

The last major speech that Elijah Muhammad was to give as Messenger of the Nation of Islam was optimistic in tone and content. Speaking to the 1974 Saviour's Day audience, he called for mutual respect amongst Muslims, and

---

[92]See, for example, *Muhammad Speaks* January 26, 1973, p. 15, and February 9, 1973, p. 18.

[93] *The New York Times*, May 3, 1973, p. 26.

[94] *The New York Times*, September 8, 1973, p. 68. The conflict at the Newark Temple was particularly violent. After the death of Shabazz, four other men were murdered. *The New York Times*, October 19, 1973, p. 47, and October 25, 1973, p. 32.

[95] *The Chicago Tribune*, January 28, 1973, p. 7.

discussed the need for respect between his followers and Whites:

> This I mean from my heart; everywhere we go respect people and
> people will respect you. Don't think that you're so great now just
> because God promised you the Kingdom; wait until you get in.[96]

Although Elijah repeated his demand for a separate state[97] and remained firm
in his distinguishing of the races, (Whites "were made to hide the reality
of God ...."),[98] much of the anger of the Muslims' early rhetoric was gone.
Indeed, at this Saviour's Day meeting, Elijah allowed Whites to share the
podium with him.[99] The self-sufficiency the Muslims had achieved allowed a
new interpretation of their existence. Elijah stated:

> I SAY THAT the Black man in North America has nobody to
> blame but himself. If he respects himself and will do for himself,
> his once slavemaster will come and respect him and help him to do
> something for self.[100]

This somewhat more conciliatory attitude towards American society was evidenced in the Muslims' activities later in 1974, and early in the following
year. The January 1975 editions of *Muhammad Speaks* featured stories that
concerned the interaction of the Muslim community with a variety of Christian denominations.[101] As well, the Nation's commitment to the larger Black

---

[96]*Muhammad Speaks*, March 28, 1975, p. 11.

[97]*Ibid.* p. 14.

[98]*Ibid.*

[99]Interview with Imam Nuri Muhammad, Associate Editor, *The Muslim Journal*, May 19,
1986.

[100]*Muhammad Speaks*, March 28, 1975, p. 14.

[101]See, for example, "Muslim Minister Enlivens Tenn. Church", *Muhammad Speaks*, January
3, 1975, p. 5.

community was reinforced in an article that discussed Muslim aid (the Committee on Cleanliness) to the tenants of a Philadelphia housing project.[102] The respect that Elijah Muhammad had deemed to be of central importance to the Muslims' future also appeared to have developed.

The early weeks of 1975 saw Elijah Muhammad's health worsen considerably; on January 30, he entered Chicago's Mercy Hospital. Perhaps in response to this, many civic authorities sought to honour his achievements. The mayor of Chicago, Richard Daley, proclaimed Saviour's Day (February 26) 1975 to be Nation of Islam Day throughout Chicago, and the mayors of Oakland, Berkeley, Los Angeles, Gary, Newark, and Atlanta followed with similar honours, making specific reference to the work of Elijah Muhammad.[103] As the *Chicago Defender* noted:

> Through the Muslim teachings, thousands of persons have been redeemed from lives of crime, drug addiction, and degradation.
>
> While we may not all agree with the ideology of the Muslim religion, we acknowledge that it has raised the principle of self development to a new high.[104]

Saviour's Day 1975 saw over 25,000 Muslims gather in Chicago; their number was testimony to the compelling nature and staying power of the Nation of Islam doctrine. On the eve of their meeting (February 25), Elijah Muhammad, Messenger of Allah, died.

---

[102] *Muhammad Speaks*, January 24, 1975, p. 5.

[103] *Muhammad Speaks*, February 14, 1975, p. 3.

[104] *The Chicago Defender*, as quoted in *Muhammad Speaks*, February 28, 1975, p. 5.

Chapter 4

WALLACE'S LEADERSHIP: THE MUSLIMS'DOCTRINE IS DE-ESCHATOLOGIZED

Brother and Sister, you can now put down the walking cane of 'blackness' and stop putting on excuses for being crippled. Strong men and strong women don't want excuses like skin color.[1]

Wallace D. Muhammad

The death of Elijah Muhammad marked the end of an era for the Nation of Islam. Under him the Nation had established itself, endured crises, and prospered. While the loss of the Messenger's leadership was a great tragedy for his followers, it also afforded the movement a valuable opportunity. The 1970s held the promise of a better future for Blacks, and the stable atmosphere this provided made the anger and hatred of the doctrine seem in many ways anachronistic. Elijah Muhammad had led the Nation through a difficult and

---

[1] Wallace Muhammad, *Muhammad Speaks*, July 18, 1975, p. S-2.

turbulent period in the history of American race relations, and his message had been in some ways an appropriate and powerful statement during that time. For the United States and for the Nation itself, however, a new age seemed to have arrived, and a new leader could more easily introduce new beliefs. The time had come for a complete de-eschatologizing of the Nation's doctrine.

The gap left by Elijah was large; as both leader and divine Messenger he seemed irreplaceable. Many possible candidates for his position had emerged in the 1970s, but no obvious choice existed. Media speculation of factionalism within the movement was therefore rampant in the weeks preceding Elijah Muhammad's death. The change in leadership occurred without incident, however. Wallace Muhammad, Elijah's seventh child, was named by him as his successor, and a committee composed of members of Elijah Muhammad's family and Muhammad Ali oversaw the transition.[2] Wallace's appointment was announced by National Secretary Abass Rassoull on Saviour's Day, February 26, 1975, one day after Elijah Muhammad's passing.[3]

Wallace Muhammad was in many ways a surprising choice for the new position of Supreme Minister of the Nation of Islam. (As Elijah Muhammad had been the divine Messenger of Allah, no other individual could assume his title.) One perhaps would have expected the leadership to fall to Elijah's eldest son, an individual more entrenched in the Muslim hierarchy, or at least an individual with a history of consistent loyalty to that hierarchy. Although educated at the Chicago University of Islam, and a member and one-time lieutenant of the Fruit of Islam,[4] Wallace had less public exposure than many other members, and had a turbulent history within the movement. During the 1960s, he was heavily influenced by Malcolm X, and he apparently questioned

---

[2] *The Chicago Tribune*, February 26, 1975, p. 15.

[3] *Muhammad Speaks*, March 14, 1975, p. 3.

[4] *Muhammad Speaks* March 21, 1975, p. 11.

his father's interpretation of Islam as early as 1961.[5] Indeed, Wallace left the movement at approximately the same time as did Malcolm X and established the short-lived Afro-Descendant Society of Upliftment. [6] He rejoined the Nation in early 1965, after Malcolm's assassination, only to be suspended once again.[7] In 1969 Wallace was again admitted back into the movement, but he did not regain his status as a Minister until 1974.[8]

Close examination of the Nation's activities and doctrine in the early 1970s help to make the choice and acceptance of Wallace as successor more understandable. As noted above, the 1970s had seen a gradual lessening of the Muslims' white devil rhetoric, a stronger emphasis on the study of the Qur'an, and a greater effort made to improve the Nation's contacts with communities outside its own. His history within the movement and his apparent belief in a more orthodox form of Islam made Wallace representative of this changed tone in the Nation. It is clear from his speech at Saviour's Day, 1975, and from concurrent articles in *Muhammad Speaks* that Wallace not only accepted these changes but was impatient to make formal alterations in the Nation's doctrine.[9]

Wallace presented his leadership as being preordained by Allah. He explained:

> It was God's plan. But I have also heard my Father, Himself, say
> that when I was born or when I was conceived in my mother. He

---

[5]C. Marsh, *From Black Muslims to Muslims, The Transition from Separatism to Islam, 1930-1980* (Metuchen: The Scarecrow Press, 1984), pp. 69-76.

[6]*The Chicago Tribune*, March 2, 1975, p. 4.

[7]C. Marsh, *From Black Muslims to Muslims*, p. 90.

[8]*Ibid.*

[9]See for example, "First Official Interview with the Supreme Minister of the Nation of Islam, the Honorable Wallace D. Muhammad," *Muhammad Speaks*, March 21, 1975, pp. 3-14.

had been born as the Servant, the Messenger of God, who manifested Himself with W.F. Muhammad; and by me being born at the
time when He was in contact with His Saviour, the God in Person,
helped to form me, not only as a child of His loins, but a child for
the Mission.[10]

The show of support given Wallace at his first Saviour's Day as Supreme
Minister was impressive; many of the most important members of the Na-
tion, including Raymond Sharrieff and Louis Farrakhan formally "verified their
allegiance"[11] to the new leader. Other dignitaries in attendance praised Elijah
Muhammad's achievements and predicted continued success for the Nation.
Jesse Jackson stated:

I sat at the Messenger's feet and was taught. The Honorable Elijah
Muhammad was the father of Black consciousness."[12]

Muhammad Sharieff, a professor from Norfolk State College, predicted that in
the future "the Nation of Islam will grow even more viable and stronger. The
Messenger has taught his followers well."[13] One hint of discontent was evident,
however. The *Chicago Tribune* noted that Herbert Muhammad, Wallace's
brother, was "conspicuously absent from speech-making,"[14] and intimated that
some type of private arrangement had been made by which Herbert was to be
in charge of "behind the scenes activity."[15] The overriding impression that
emerged from this Saviour's Day meeting, though, is one of a strongly unified

---

[10]*Muhammad Speaks*, March 21, 1975, p. 3.

[11]*Muhammad Speaks*, March 14, 1975, p. 3.

[12]*Ibid.*, p. 5.

[13]*Ibid.*

[14]*The Chicago Tribune*, February 27, 1975, II, p. 1.

[15]*Ibid.*

Nation. The movement had survived its most serious crisis ever and appeared well-equipped to face the challenges of the future. One of the most concise statements of this assessment was quoted in the *Chicago Tribune.* A bank official was heard to remark, "The new leadership is not expected to threaten the empire's excellent credit rating." [16]

The first years of Wallace Muhammad's leadership can best be described as a time of change. While Elijah was alive, his prophecy of the Fall of America could be reinterpreted and pushed farther into the future. With his death, the doctrine itself was more likely to be questioned, especially in light of the socio-economic shift within the group, and the changed context in which it operated. In response to this Wallace Muhammad moved the Nation of Islam from a doctrine of political millenarianism to Orthodox Islam. The alterations that he made in the Nation's political and religious beliefs completed the process of de-eschatologizing that was begun during his father's lifetime.

The transformation of the movement took place in two waves. The first set of changes initiated by Wallace was undoubtedly the most startling. They were invoked almost immediately following his ascension to the leadership and drastically altered the Nation's doctrine. The second wave of changes shaped the now moderate group of Muslims into an Islamic community. They were made over a longer period of time and completed the group's metamorphosis.

Wallace began his years as Supreme Minister still very much under the shadow of his father, a situation which while perhaps constricting, gave greater legitimacy to his actions; many of the changes instituted by him were explained as having their origins with Elijah. [17] As discussed above, this connection does

---

[16] *The Chicago Tribune*, March 2, 1975, p. 4.

[17] For example, in "First Official Interview with the Supreme Minister of the Nation of Islam, Wallace D. Muhammad," Wallace hints that before his death Elijah Muhammad was changing his attitude towards Whites. *Muhammad Speaks*, March 21, 1975, p. 12.

not seem to be a fabrication. Saviour's Day 1974 saw the Messenger allow Whites on the podium beside him,[18] and his sermon on that day was notable for its tone of moderation.[19]

Wallace's first attempt to reshape the Nation was a general reinterpretation of its role in the world and its meaning in history. He began by elaborating upon his father's doctrine of the "Resurrection" of Black Americans. In a series of articles in *Muhammad Speaks*, Wallace detailed the new doctrine of the Second Resurrection.[20] Once again, the Book of Revelation was used to analyze the history of Blacks in the United States.

> There are revealing parallels in the study of Christ's life and death and the study of our former life as a people and our death as a people in the West. These parallels are seen further in his scriptural resurrection and our resurrection as a people in the body – Christ of the Second Coming, which is the Nation of Islam. The Second Coming of Christ is a gift of a community by or from the Divine Hand. Revelations [sic] 21:1-3.[21]

The Second Resurrection, however, was no longer to be interpreted as an apocalyptic event of the future. Rather, it was now to be seen as a mission. In this way, Wallace Muhammad successfully de-eschatologized the Muslims' doctrine.

Wallace did not attempt to sever all ties with the work of his father. Elijah Muhammad was interpreted as having achieved the "First Resurrection" of Black Americans:

---

[18]Interview with Imam Nuri Muhammad, Assoc. Editor of the *Muslim Journal*, May 19, 1986.

[19]"The Last Sermon" is reprinted in *Muhammad Speaks*, March 14, 1975, pp. 11-14.

[20]The articles ran from April 11 through April 25, 1975.

[21]*Muhammad Speaks*, May 2, 1975, p. 1.

> In the First Resurrection God began to raise us up out of the graves
> by beginning to unveil the Truth. In the Second Resurrection the
> Truth is not just unveiled in a sense of scriptural interpretation,
> but we come to a kind of natural interpretation ... We have been
> taught many things in the Teachings of the Great Master W.F.
> Muhammad and the Honorable Master Elijah Muhammad that
> have prepared us for this time ... [22]

Underlining the political nature of the Muslims' former doctrine, he noted,
"We now have the power to move on earth as a people. Our new birth into
the Total Light of Divine makes the world recognize us for the first time as a
people." [23] With pride and knowledge of self, the Muslims could now begin their
true mission, "to light the world and to deliver it from darkness, backwardness,
and human poverty." [24]

Important aspects of the doctrine were specifically reinterpreted. Elijah's
interpretation of Ezekiel's Wheel, for example, was completely de-eschatologized.
No longer was the Wheel the initiator of the apocalypse. Wallace wrote:

> Ezekiel saw this body as a wheel (Nation of Islam) in a wheel (world
> community), the Revelator saw it as a city manifested down from
> the sky, indicating a divinely revealed community. [25]

Much as Augustine had interpreted the New Testament to view the Christian Church as the embodiment of the Kingdom of God on Earth, [26] Wallace

---

[22] *Muhammad Speaks*, April 11, 1975, p. 13.

[23] *Ibid.*, p. 12.

[24] *Ibid.*, p. 13.

[25] *Muhammad Speaks*, May 9, 1975, p. 1.

[26] E. Benz, *Evolution and Christian Hope*, Trans. H.G. Frank, (Garden City: Anchor Books, 1968), p. 23.

changed an apocalyptic vision of Ezekiel's Wheel into one in which it was the embodiment of a divinely revealed community. By thus interpreting the Nation as having partially fulfilled its role in raising Black consciousness and moving Blacks toward Islam, Wallace effectively tied the history of the Nation to the Black movement and at the same time allowed it to become an established religious community.[27]

This new interpretation of the Muslims' doctrine initiated what some have termed the "rebirth of the Nation." In his first public address after Saviour's Day, Wallace spoke to over twenty-five thousand Blacks in Philadelphia, delivering a lecture entitled "Remake the World."[28] Although he spoke of many topics during his speech, one in particular stood out: The Mission of the Nation of Islam. In the past, the Nation had concentrated on the development of Black Americans. Through economic and social programs, it had been extremely successful in working towards this goal. Although Elijah Muhammad had indeed achieved an empire, he had isolated his people. Their separation from the outside world was desirable when they lacked a sense of community and when the Fall of America appeared imminent. When the eschaton was reinterpreted however, it became more a hindrance than a help. Elijah had raised Black consciousness in terms of knowledge of self, and in doing so had created a community able to withstand and even prosper within the huge empire that surrounded it. When the Chosen People became merely a religious

---

[27]Much as reborn Christians emphasize a return to the experience of God, in the early stages of the "Second Resurrection" Wallace emphasized a vision of God that allowed a clearer interpretation of Scripture. Guided by him, Muslims could come to see "the light behind the veil," *Muhammad Speaks*, April 11, 1975, pp. 12-13. This parallel is interesting, for the primal religious experience of Christianity is, along with millenarianism, a means by which a movement can, in Anthony Wallace's terms, become revitalized.

For the Muslims, this flirtation with experiential religion was brief. After emphasizing the new doctrine for a period sufficient to insure its general acceptance, Wallace began to stress the scripture of the Qur'an.

[28]*Muhammad Speaks*, May 9, 1975, p. 3.

community, so too did their mission change. Their focus was no longer introspective, rather they were to share their knowledge with the community of Man. Wallace wrote:

> The Mission of the Nation of Islam is to restore the total man, the total life, the total community. Pollution of land, air, and sea is a problem for this world, but it doesn't discourage us. We are not going to give up the city and go to some artificial garden of Eden to eat wild berries, to wear sneakers, and long beards, and to go without baths. We haven't given up on civilization – we started it. We're going to give it birth again and keep it going.[29]

This new mission indirectly demanded of the Muslims that particular aspects of their doctrine be altered. Among these was one of the most controversial tenets of their religious doctrine: their judgment of Whites as being intrinsically evil, or devils.

There were many hints preceding Wallace's formal announcement of change that pointed to the imminent rejection of this assessment of Whites. In the May 16, 1975, issue of *Muhammad Speaks* Wallace wrote,

> I'm not calling those people [Whites] "devil." I'm calling the mind that has ruled those people and you "devil." It ruled them for their glory and ruled you for your shame.[30]

The revitalized Nation emerged at Chicago's McCormick Place on June 15, 1975.[31] In a meeting open to the general public,[32] Wallace lectured on

---

[29] *Muhammad Speaks*, May 23, 1975, p. 16.

[30] *Muhammad Speaks*, May 16, 1975, p. 13.

[31] *Muhammad Speaks*, July 4, 1975, p. 1.

[32] *Ibid.*, p. S-4.

"Religion Means Alive," and for the first time in the Nation's history, made public the financial structure and membership figures of the organization. [33] This new openness was echoed in the Nation's religious doctrine as well.

With the statement, "What was good teaching for yesterday was good for yesterday ... the same is not good for today,"[34] Wallace initiated perhaps the most radical change possible in the Muslims' doctrine. A short one hundred days after his father's death, he announced "from now on whites will be considered fully human."[35] All men were now to be accepted in God's community. No longer was the term "white devil" to be used to refer to Caucasians, and from that time onward, Whites were to be permitted and encouraged to join the Nation.[36] In a later article in *Muhammad Speaks* Wallace explained:

> You can destroy a devil by destroying the mind that the person
> has grown within them. If you can destroy the mind, you will
> destroy the devil ... Today the Nation of Islam (the body-Christ)
> is destroying the devil without hands by casting him into our Lake
> of Fire (Divine Truth and Knowledge).[37]

The only devil to be conquered now was ignorance.[38]

Although there had been as yet no outward expression of dissatisfaction within the Nation, rumours of a rift in the movement had persisted. The Nation's hierarchy grasped the opportunity offered by this June meeting to

---

[33] *Muhammad Speaks*, July 4, 1975, p. 1.

[34] *Ibid.*, p. 3.

[35] *Time*, June 30, 1975, p. 44.

[36] *The New York Times.*, p. 9. It is interesting to note that these changes are not directly discussed in *Muhammad Speaks*. This omission is perhaps due to a desire to keep disruption within the Nation to a minimum.

[37] *Muhammad Speaks*, July 11, 1975, p. 13.

[38] *Ibid.*, p. 14.

formally address the issue. Minister Farrakhan, perhaps the focus of many of these rumours, addressed the question directly:

> Certain writers who were amazed and angered at the smooth tran-
> sition of power in the Nation of Islam, have created a power struggle
> with their pens. We laugh at their futile attempt like it is a joke.[39]

To this he added, "No ill winds will ruffle the shades of this divine nation. No one among us is high enough to tie the shoelaces of Wallace."[40] With a solid organizational basis, an apparently increasing membership, and the planned construction of a new nursing home and preschool centre, the Nation appeared to be rising above even its past achievements.[41]

In an apparent effort to consolidate acceptance of the changes he had made, Wallace travelled to New York on June 29 to speak at Madison Square Garden.[42] Over forty thousand people attended the event, and "millions more" were able to view it on television.[43] The meeting could perhaps best be de-scribed as an extravaganza celebrating the "new" Nation. The mayor had proclaimed the day "Muhammad Appreciation Day," and many civic digni-taries attended the meeting, as did representatives from over thirty nations. Perhaps the most important visitor was Amabassador Amin Hilmy II, from the League of Arab States;[44] his presence was an expression of tacit approval of the Nation by the Muslim countries of the Middle East.

---

[39] *Muhammad Speaks*, July 4, 1975, p. 3.

[40] *The Chicago Tribune*, June 16, 1975, p. 3.

[41] *Ibid.*

[42] *Muhammad Speaks*, July 18, 1975, p. 4.

[43] The Public Broadcasting System in the United States carried a two and one half hour special which included much of the Supreme Minister's speech as well as a discussion panel on the Nation.

[44] *Muhammad Speaks*, July 18, 1975, p. 4.

Although Wallace's speech was, for the most part, a reiteration of the recent doctrinal changes, one significant announcement was made. Amongst the many positive events that occurred in New York, it was a sharp reminder that old beliefs cannot be merely pushed aside. Minister Abdul Haleem Farrakhan was abruptly transferred from the powerful Harlem Mosque to the Nation's offices in Chicago. Wallace stated that this transfer was in actuality a promotion,[45] but it seemed suspiciously like a means of more closely supervising Farrakhan.[46]

These doctrinal changes were reflected in the Muslims' literature and way of life. In response to this changed Nation, the Muslims' publication, *Muhammad Speaks*, also began to have a more outward-looking perspective. For example, the world of popular music was for the first time examined in a positive light. Stevie Wonder, who had that year dedicated his seven Grammy Awards to the memory of Elijah Muhammad, was featured in a June edition of the paper.[47]

Two events held later that summer underlined the changing nature of the Nation. The first was a command performance by the group Kool and the Gang at the Muhammad residence in Chicago.[48] Although the group had written a number of compositions based on the Nation, and indeed some members were Muslims, their performance at Elijah's former home was unprecedented.

The second controversial event was held in late August. *The Chicago Tribune* wrote:

Nothing has been so symbolic of the rapid changes within the Nation of Islam since the death of its founder than the interracial

---

[45]*Muhammad Speaks*, July 18, 1975, p. S-1.

[46]One of Farrakhan's first duties in his new position was to travel to Uganda to speak at Mukerere University and meet with Idi Amin. His speech at that time emphasized the older doctrine of the Nation.

[47]*Muhammad Speaks*, June 6, 1975, p. 23.

[48]*Muhammad Speaks*, August 8, 1975.

"beautiful people" party [recently] held ...[49]

The party, given for Muhammad Ali, was a lavish affair, attended by a number of celebrities, among them Stevie Wonder, Lola Falana, and Jesse Jackson.[50] Although serious matters were attended to (Jesse Jackson received a ten thousand dollar cheque for Operation PUSH, and a one hundred thousand dollar cheque was given to UNICEF for Sahara drought relief), the party was an event unequalled in the history of the Muslims; for the first time at a Nation of Islam function dancing and smoking were permitted.[51] Although one member was heard to remark joyfully, "It's boogie time in the Nation,"[52] his enthusiasm was not shared by all his Brothers. Many began to predict that such rapid changes to the Muslims' faith were bound to cause difficulties.

The last major change initiated by Wallace in 1975 occurred in late September. The American Blacks' struggle to define their community had long suffered because of the lack of an appropriate vocabulary. Appellations thrust upon them by the ruling White majority had been generally prejudicial and, not surprisingly, disliked. The term "Black" embodied a sense of historical glory and suffering, and emerging power, but its meaning was found in the political realm. A religious community required a terminology with spiritual significance. In an effort to remedy this situation, Wallace turned to the history of Islam. He chose the term Bilalian, derived from the name of Bilal Ibn Rabah, to represent the American Black community.[53] The slave Bilal, by his life and spiritual conviction, symbolized their historical experience, and provided

---

[49] *The Chicago Tribune*, Sept. 1, 1975, p. 1.

[50] *Ibid.*

[51] *Ibid. The Chicago Tribune* added, somewhat smugly, "a White public relations firm handled the $100,000 affair," *Ibid.*, p. 13).

[52] *The New York Times*, Sept. 1, p. 13.

[53] *Muhammad Speaks*, Oct. 24, 1975, p. 2.

a model of religious devotion for them to strive for. Muhammad Abdul-Rauf writes that Bilal

> rose through his faith to the highest degree of honor and distinction
> despite the position society had placed him in. Bilal's strength was
> in his solid conviction which sustained him in the savage persecution
> meted out to him by his oppressive master. Ultimately Bilal was
> delivered and his master ended in an ignominious humiliation and
> disgraceful death.[54]

This change in name was an important step for the Nation; by overriding their identity as Americans it drew the Muslims closer yet to Orthodox Islam. In response to this new interpretation of their communal identity, the Muslims renamed *Muhammad Speaks*. On November 14, 1975, the first issue of the *Bilalian News* appeared. With its inception the weekly publication of "What the Muslims Want" was discontinued, (see Appendix One).

On February 1, 1976, the rebuilt Temple in Harlem was renamed Malcolm Shabazz Temple 7 for the once-disowned Malcolm X,[55] thus restoring the dissident's place in the Nation's history. This move, largely symbolic, ushered in another year of change in the Nation.

Later in February, Wallace made other drastic changes to the Nation's creed, all of which continued its evolution into a mainstream religious community. One of the first was a formal denunciation of the Nation's demand for land. Wallace stated, "My father was bluffing when he talked about a separate state. He knew he could never get it, but he saw no harm in asking."[56] Like

---

[54]M. Abdul-Rauf, *Bilal Ibn Rabah*, (Maryland: American Trust Publications, 1977), p. 1.

[55]*New York Times*, Feb. 2, 1976, p. 1.

[56]J.E. Whitehurst, "The Mainstreaming of the Black Muslims," *Christian Century*, February 27, 1980, p. 226.

the Fall of America, the demand for a separate state was now interpreted as a means for motivating Blacks. In February too, Dr. Naim Ak'bar announced that a number of Whites had been admitted to the Nation.[57] The *Chicago Tribune* remarked that no exact membership figure was made public, but under the circumstances that criticism was irrelevant. What mattered was that, aside from its movement towards Orthodox Islam, the Nation had also begun the process of integration with the White population.

The Nation of Islam at Saviour's Day 1976 was vastly different than it had been only a year before. The Muslims were now clearly a religious, rather than political group. Reflecting this changed nature the meeting was, for the first time, held in a temple.[58] Wallace encouraged his fellow Muslims to become actively involved in politics, and for the first time the American flag flew above a Muslim meeting.[59] Repeating his openness of the year before, Wallace announced that the Nation was in debt over four and half million dollars, an amount which, although reduced from its 1973 nine million dollar peak, was still overwhelming.[60] Related to this, the *Chicago Tribune* noted:

> In what appeared to be a crackdown on reported criminal offences in the Nation, Muhammad said, "From now on all ministers will be removed from business operations. There have been abuses, many of them because the ministers were desparate in their attempts to keep money flowing back to Chicago.[61]

The appearance of a financially sound business empire was to be sacrificed

---

[57] *Chicago Tribune*, Feb. 19, 1976, II, p. 1.

[58] *Chicago Tribune*, Feb. 19, 1976, II, p. 1.

[59] D.A. Williams and E. Sciolino, "Rebirth of the Nation," *Newsweek*, March 10, 1976, p. 33.

[60] *Chicago Tribune*, March 1, 1976, p. 1.

[61] *Ibid.*

in the creation of a stable religious community.

On a more positive note, it was announced at this meeting that membership in the Nation had risen during 1975,[62] a fact that seemed to indicate that the moderate doctrine was beginning to capture larger sectors of the Black middle class. This apparent movement of the Nation towards the middle class was echoed in another change in policy made at this Saviour's Day meeting. Of seemingly little immediate importance, it was a powerful indicator of the changed composition of the Nation and its mission: from that time onward, the Nation was no longer to pay the legal fees of members charged with criminal offences.[63]

In March of 1976 Wallace made yet another alteration in the Muslims' doctrine; he announced that no longer would his father be interpreted as being the last Messenger of Allah, [64] for "Wallace felt his father had not been speaking in the theological spirit of the Koran and Bible."[65] Elijah was now to be considered a wise man who brought American Blacks to the Qur'an, and Wallace Fard was to be interpreted as merely the founder of the movement.[66] Wallace stated, "I want to get rid of all this spiritual spookiness."[67] The magnitude of this change in the Nation's doctrine is undeniable, yet in the context of Wallace's previous changes, it is almost unsurprising.

Later in the year the Nation proceeded with programs based on the policy changes Wallace had announced at Saviour's Day. In May, the Muslims took

---

[62] *Chicago Tribune*, March 1, 1976, p. 1.

[63] *New York Times*, Feb. 26, 1976, p. 14.

[64] *Chicago Tribune*, March 7, 1976, p. 38.

[65] C. Marsh, *From Black Muslims to Muslims*, p. 93.

[66] *Ibid.*

[67] *Chicago Tribune*, March 7, 1976, p. 38.

part in a program aimed at the mass registration of Black voters,[68] and in August the Nation responded to its grim financial situation. Wallace began to dismantle the business empire that had taken Elijah Muhammad over forty years to build.

The second, less radical wave of changes that Wallace was to initiate began later that year. On October 18, the Nation of Islam became the World Community of al-Islam in the West, (WCIW).[69] Wallace made this change in order that the group's name more accurately reflect its intent.

> We're a world community – a community that encompasses every-
> body. We have Caucasians and Orientals who are members and we
> are all just Muslims.[70]

Indeed, this change seemed largely cosmetic: the circumstances underlying it had occurred much earlier. Like the change from Blacks to Bilalians, this new name for the Nation reinforced its role as a religious community.

The last major changes initiated by Wallace occurred in the early months of 1977. The first was surprising only in that it had not been instituted earlier. The Muslims' Temples were to be renamed Masjids, bringing the American community in line with the rest of the Muslim world.[71] The second alteration made that year was perhaps no less inevitable, but its effect was more widely felt. The Fruit of Islam, the Muslims' private police force, was abolished, thus effectively removing the last traces of the movement's original political identity. Despite these final changes, the remainder of 1977 was quiet for the Muslims. The one notable event of that year was Wallace's campaign to bring

---

[68] *New York Times*, May 7, 1976, II, p. 5.

[69] *New York Times*, Oct. 19, 1976, p. 33.

[70] *Ibid.*

[71] *Time*, March 14, 1977.

the problems of America's urban ghettos to the attention of the White House. This program gathered momentum as the year progressed, and culminated in a meeting of the Supreme Minister and President Jimmy Carter, an event the *Bilalian News* commented "few would have thought likely as recently as four years ago."[72] After the abrupt series of changes which it had undergone, the Muslim community appeared to be stabilizing.

This was not the case, however. Early in January of 1978, it became evident that serious problems existed within the organization. New York's *Amsterdam News* carried a front-page story that month concerning a "split" between Wallace Muhammad and Louis Farrakhan; the problem was now too large for the Muslims to hide. The *Chicago Tribune* noted that story, and contacted both Wallace's representative, who replied that nothing was wrong, and Louis Farrakhan, who stated flatly, "I am not welcomed in the World Community of Al-Islam in the West and I know it." [73] The *New York Times* reported that the movement

> had lost thousands of members and [was] struggling to stave off an
> ideological cleavage that could further polarize its followers.[74]

Minister Farrakhan announced to the *New York Times* on March 7, 1978 that he was severing all ties with Wallace Muhammad's World Community of Islam.[75] Twelve days later he made public his plans to rebuild the Nation of

---

[72] *Bilalian News*, Jan. 20., 1978, p. 4

[73] *The Chicago Tribune*, January 20, 1978, III, p. 4.

[74] *The New York Times*, March 7, 1978, p. 18.

[75] *The New York Times*, March 7, 1978, p. 18. It should be noted that the exact date of Farrakhan's departure from the WCIW is unclear. Abdul Wali Muhammad of the *Final Call* stated that Farrakhan actually left in September of 1977. At a press conference in Hollywood, the Minister had announced he would "stand up and rebuild the Nation." Interview with Abdul Wali Muhammad, Editor, *The Final Call*, May 23, 1986.

Islam; discipline and separatism were to be reinstated.[76]

Although it is likely Farrakhan's leavetaking caused some disruption, it seems probable that the movement was not as badly off as media reports indicated. Undoubtedly many members were dissatisfied, to varying degrees, with Wallace's changes to the doctrine. Their dissatisfaction, however, did not seem to be an active force in the movement at this time.[77]

Wallace Muhammad responded to Louis Farrakhan's departure in a speech on March 24. His appeal was an accurate statement of his disagreement with Farrakhan. He requested that those loyal to him neither picket Farrakhan's meetings nor challenge him publicly, and even offered the Minister the Harlem Mosque again.[78] Ever conscious of the possibility of factionalism within the community, and likely with the memory of Malcolm X's assassination haunting him, Wallace stated:

> Who is it now that's so anxious to make Minister Farrakhan a great
>
> public figure and challenge the WCIW? Who is anxious to do this?
>
> It's the people who want to destroy us, not Farrakhan.[79]

The harshest criticism that Wallace made of Farrakhan in this speech was that the latter was "not going to change the world of the racists and the separatists."[80] Retreating to the original beliefs of the Nation and without the

---

[76] *The New York Times*, March 19, 1978, p. 37.

[77] Both Imam Nuri Muhammad of the *Muslim Journal* and Abdul Wali Muhammad of the *Final Call* stressed in their interviews with me that Farrakhan's departure from the WCIW in no way represented a "split" in the movement. Minister Farrakhan left the group, and individuals so desiring joined him. Although this is perhaps a somewhat idealized version of an historical event, it seems grounded in truth; there were no outbreaks of violence (as occurred in the early 1970s), and there were no inflammatory public statements made by either leader. Interview with Imam Nuri Muhammad, Assoc. Editor of the *Muslim Journal*, May 19, 1986. Interview with Abdul Wali Muhammad, Editor, *The Final Call*, May 23, 1986.

[78] *Bilalian News*, April 28, 1978, p. 23.

[79] *Ibid.*

[80] *Ibid.*

guidance of Islam, Farrakhan's followers would be limited in spiritual growth, and thus in other areas, for example the economic realm. Minister Farrakhan refused the Supreme Minister's offer of the Harlem Mosque, and began to rebuild the Nation of Islam as Elijah Muhammad had known it. Under the leadership of a very outspoken and controversial leader, the "new" Nation of Islam has prospered. The development of this group, and its millenarian beliefs, will be discussed below.

Within the WCIW, more changes occurred in 1978. Saviour's Day, previously one of the Muslims' most important meetings, was replaced by Ethnic Survival Week,[81] a celebration of the achievements of Black Americans. In a similar move, Wallace that year created New World Patriotism Day, to be observed on Independence Day, July 4. The *Bilalian News* wrote:

> This was another great and significant move in the reformation of the [WCIW's] membership into oustanding examples of model American citizens.[82]

Later in 1978, Wallace ordered a major restructuring of the WCIW bureaucracy. On September 10, he announced his resignation to an Atlanta audience, stating that he wanted to travel as the community's ambassador and fulfill an "evangelistic mission."[83] From that point on, the Muslim community was to be led by a democratically elected council of six Imams.[84] As his final request, Wallace asked that the Council attempt to preserve "Koranic purity" and "pledge itself to a capitalistic form of business."[85]

---

[81] *Bilalian News*, March 3, 1978, p. 3.

[82] *Ibid.*

[83] *Chicago Tribune*, Sept. 13, 1978, III, p. 1.

[84] *Ibid.* Despite this resignation, Wallace has remained a central figure in the group.

[85] *Ibid.*

The next years were quiet ones for the American Muslim community. The time was marked by few notable incidents, but scattered with events reflecting the changed nature of the group. The degree to which the Bilalians had abandoned Elijah Muhammad's political principles was made evident in January of 1979. Following their first leader's vision of an economically self-sufficient Black community, the Muslims had developed an efficient independent food service industry. Their company, Salaam International, in conjunction with another Chicago firm, signed a twenty-two million dollar contract with the United States Department of National Defence.[86] This arrangement, while creating four hundred jobs in Chicago's South Side, represented a political role for the Muslims that the original Nation of Islam would never have engaged in.[87]

That same month, evidence of Elijah Muhammad's very mortal qualities was brought into the open. Settlement of the Messenger's estate began in 1979; aside from his eight children by Clara, fifteen illegitimate children were named as heirs. Elijah fathered the children by eight women who were employed as secretaries in his home.[88] To the press, Emmanuel Muhammad stated that his father "had bought houses for each of the eight secretaries, had enrolled their children in the Muslim school, and had provided financial support when requested."[89] The information that had fostered Malcolm X's disillusionment with the movement was now public knowledge.

1980 was another uneventful year for the Muslim community, but two events of note did occur. Wallace announced a change in name in the March 14 issue of the *Bilalian News*; he was now to be known as Warith Deen Muhammad.

---

[86] J.E. Whitehurst, "The Mainstreaming of the Black Muslims," p. 229.

[87] *Chicago Tribune*, Jan. 7, 1979, p. 6.

[88] *Ibid.*

[89] *Ibid.*

This change to an Islamic name represented another move to Orthodox Islam.[90] According to Warith, the new name meant "Inheritor of the faith of Muhammad."

The following month, he instituted another name change for the community. The World Community of al-Islam in the West became simply the American Muslim Mission.[91] He explained:

> The Quranic term for Mission is 'DA-WAH' ... Literally, the term
> Da-wah signifies involvement in those concerns affecting the life of
> society, and the need to stay on top of the issues ... Nations and
> communities come and go, Da-wah is continuous.[92]

Rather than a community of Muslims separated by their citizenship in the Western World, and having a mission defined by that environment, the Muslims were now to be considered part of the wider Islamic community, fulfilling a common mission in a specific geographical area.[93] With this change in name the *Bilalian News* became the *American Muslim Journal*.

Illustrating the group's transition from radical millenarianism to mainline religious community is the lack of press coverage given the movement during the 1980s. Abrubtly, stories concerning Warith's Muslim community are nowhere to be found, while Louis Farrakhan and the Nation of Islam are frequently reported in national newspapers. Indeed, the most recent history of the Muslim community must be traced through its own publications.

For the Muslim community the period of 1980 through 1986 was marked by no spectacular events. Indeed, of any era in its history, these years are undoubt-

---

[90]*Bilalian News*, March 14, 1980, p. 3.

[91]*Bilalian News*, May 16, 1980, p. 2.

[92]*Bilalian News*, May 23, 1980, p. 2.

[93]It should be noted that despite this name change, the American community retained the name Bilalians.

edly the group's most peaceful. Perhaps a response to the rapid transformation that had occurred in the 1970s, this period must be interpreted as one of stabilization. Four aspects of the Muslims' creed are worth noting during this period: their attention to their identity as Blacks, their economic ventures, their political perspective, and of course, their religious faith.

As can be inferred from the discussion above, the Muslims had eliminated their emphasis on race during the first years of Wallace's leadership. Despite this, consciousness of their identity as a community within a community remained, in part because the group's membership remained predominantly Black. This aspect of its existence, while no longer the movement's focus, remained an undeniable fact. To the extent that it was relevant to their religious faith, it was expressed through action. With respect to this, two circumstances of the 1980s are important to note. The first is the Muslims' continued tie to the Black community in which it originated. Compelled by their faith to do good works in the community, the Muslims have continued to attempt improvements to America's ghettos. Through adoption programs, neighborhood clean-up programs, and other similar ventures, they have worked towards improving the social conditions of their neighbors. This emphasis is reflected in their newspaper, which reports and often highlights news specific to the Black community. Their publications often have a "Black perspective," that is, they contain critiques of society that are particularly relevant to Blacks, for example, Tony Brown's column.

The Muslims' campaign against racial images in worship reflects both their Black identity and their adherence to Islam. Their faith dictates that race is to be disregarded in one's relationship with God. As Blacks in the United States, this gives them a special mission. Every edition of their paper includes a notice highlighting this issue:

You can't live in America without hearing the message. The mes-

sage of white supremacy is everywhere. You are conscious that
Jesus is in a white body even if you don't go to church ... Every American knows that apostles and saints and angels are made
European by church society ... We are not to see God in a racial
image. As long as "white" (Caucasian) people think that their
physical image is in the world as the image of God, and as long as
non-white people see and know that the Caucasian image is in the
world as the purported image of God, there will be no real coming
together and no peaceful meeting of the minds of Caucasians and
non-Caucasians.[94]

The Muslims' new attitude towards race is constructive in their integration
with American society; it also aids in the achievement of their new vision of
the Kingdom of God on earth.

The Muslims have not neglected economic development during the 1980s.
Although their business investments have never reached the level of the early
1970s, the community has retained a number of properties. In general, the
financial investments of the group were strengthened after Wallace's stream-
lining of the business empire in 1976. An early financial venture of this period,
the American Muslim Mission Committee to Purchase 100,000 Commodities
Plus (AMMCOP), aimed at forming a buying co-operative, was unsuccessful,
however, and was dissolved in mid-1986.[95] Despite difficulties in the early
1980s, (at one point, the group's ownership of the Malcolm Shabazz Mosque in
Harlem was threatened),[96] the community at present seems financially sound.
No longer aggressively pursuing economic success, the group has in this way

---

[94]*Muslim Journal*, Aug. 15, 1986, p. 6.

[95]*Muslim Journal*, March 28, 1986.

[96]*Bilalian News*, Jan. 4, 1980, p. 30.

too become a more traditional religious organization. It has retained mosques and some other buildings, but the days of purchasing farms and banks are over.

Likewise, the Muslims have changed their political rhetoric. While integrating themselves with the larger American community through such programs as voter registration, support of particular political candidates, etc., they have at the same time remained vocal with regard to issues concerning the Black community as a whole, and have remained critical of many of the American government's policies, particularly with respect to Israel. While by no means as radical as in their early days, the Muslims have thus maintained a policy of a criticism of government and society that is rooted in their religious faith.

The doctrinal changes necessary to transform the Nation of Islam into a community practicing a more orthodox form of Islam took place during the 1970s; the 1980s have seen these changes become firmly entrenched in practice. In terms of organizational structure, two changes of note have occurred. In the spring of 1985, Wallace moved to decentralize the movement completely; at the same time, the *American Muslim Journal* became simply the *Muslim Journal*, indicating a further merging with the larger Islamic community.[97] In the spring of 1985, they began publishing *Progressions*, a monthly magazine focusing on the teachings of Islam.

Between 1975 and 1986 the Nation of Islam successfully de-eschatologized its doctrine. Wallace (Warith) Muhammad, through a rapid series of doctrinal changes, guided the movement to its present state as a religious community woven into the fabric of America. While the Muslims have been successful in making this change, Louis Farrakhan's Nation of Islam has also attracted many followers. His radical millenarian doctrine will be discussed in the following chapter.

---

[97]Interview with Imam Bilal Muhammad, Toronto, Jan. 3, 1986.

Chapter 5

THE REVITALIZATION OF THE NATION OF ISLAM

I have to do what my conscience dictates, and my conscience dictates to me that the Honorable Elijah Muhammad's plan and program for Black people is the best plan and program, and that program is an absolute necessity ... [it] needs no changes, no alteration; no one should corrupt it.[1]

Louis Farrakhan

During the first years of Wallace Muhammad's leadership of the Nation of Islam, Minister Louis Farrakhan became increasingly dissatisfied with the movement's change in direction. Although Wallace claimed to be acting upon the advice of his father and with the guidance of Allah, Louis Farrakhan could not reconcile the social condition of Black America with a religious doctrine that lacked a direct and vigorous political message. As noted above, this discontent culminated in Farrakhan's leaving the group in 1978.

---

[1]Louis Farrakhan, *The Final Call*, May, 1979, p. 13.

Minister Louis Farrakhan had always been a respected figure in the Muslim community. Lawrence Mamiya has noted that in both career and style, he closely resembles Malcolm X. [2] His oratorical gifts helped him rise quickly in the group's hierarchy, and at the time of Elijah Muhammad's death, he was one of the Messenger's most trusted advisors. It is therefore not surprising that Farrakhan, more than anyone else, felt compelled to continue the Messenger's work.

After his departure from the World Community of al-Islam in the West, Farrakhan began a cross-continental journey to Hollywood, where he intended to resume his career as a calypso singer.[3] During his trip, however, Farrakhan reread Jabril Muhammad's *This is the One*,[4] and reflected upon Elijah Muhammad's original message. In it, he found a truth still applicable to American Blacks. Rejecting Wallace Muhammad's new moderate stance, the Minister "stood back up."[5]

The Nation of Islam he subsequently built adopted the original doctrine of Elijah Muhammad, including its millenarian tenets. The myth of Yakub once again became a central tenet of belief, Elijah Muhammad's original Muslim creed (see Appendix One) was emphasized, and the eschatological vision of the Fall of America and Ezekiel's Wheel was revived. This prophecy has played a major role in the most recent history of the Nation. Its reappearance, in various forms, has marked the evolution of the movement.

Farrakhan presented the rejuvenation of the Nation of Islam as prophesied by Elijah Muhammad. He discussed this connection in the first issue of his

---

[2]L. Mamiya, "From Black Muslim to Bilalian: The Evolution of a Movement," *Journal for the Scientific Study of Religion*, 1982, 21 (2), p. 141.

[3]Interview with Abdul Wali Muhammad, Editor, *The Final Call*, May 23, 1986.

[4]The author's name at that time was Bernard Cushmeer; his book, *This is the One*, was published by the PHNX SN & Co. c. 1970.

[5]Interview with Abdul Wali Muhammad, Editor, *The Final Call*, May 23, 1986.

publication, *The Final Call.* The Honourable Elijah Muhammad allegedly stated to Minister Farrakhan in 1972:

> Brother, I don't like to talk about this because it gives me great pain but the Nation is going to take a dive for the second time ... But, don't worry Brother. It will be rebuilt and it will never fall again ... Go exactly as you see me go and do exactly as you see me do ... you must practice righteousness or they (the enemy) will piece you in two.[6]

Revealing this prophecy gave Louis Farrakhan greater legitimacy and illuminated the meaning of the movement's most recent history. The rebirth of the Nation could be understood as a religious event, rooted in the groups' origins, instead of appearing merely the result of factionalism.

Farrakhan's new organization was not composed solely of dissatisfied members of Wallace Muhammad's World Community of Al-Islam in the West. Indeed, no large migration of members between these groups has ever taken place. Rather, Farrakhan converted individuals who were completely new to the Nation of Islam, as well as those who had not been active Muslims since 1975.[7] This division of membership is very likely a contributing factor to the two groups' peaceful coexistence.

Lacking a formal organizational structure, Farrakhan began the "new" Nation by establishing study groups across the United States.[8] As the membership of these groups increased, many developed into temple communities. In 1979, the movement began publishing a paper, financed by a mortgage Louis

---

[6] *The Final Call*, May 1979, p. 3.

[7] Telephone Interview with Abdul Wali Muhammad, Editor, *The Final Call*, September 10, 1986.

[8] Interview with Abdul Wali Muhammad, Editor, *The Final Call*, May 23, 1986.

Farrakhan took out on his house. [9] The newspaper, entitled *The Final Call*, strongly emphasized the program and doctrine of Elijah Muhammad, even to its name:

> The first newspaper that the Messenger produced was in 1934 after
> His teacher Master Fard Muhammad had left Him with the Mission.
> The name of that paper was *The Final Call to Islam* ...we have
> chosen to begin as he began.[10]

The first years of the Nation's existence were quiet; Minister Farrakhan spent this period travelling across the United States lecturing to various groups. This attention to proselytizing was profitable, for when in 1981 the Nation celebrated its first Saviour's Day, between six and seven thousand people attended.[11] By 1983, the Nation of Islam had clearly established itself. Improved funding and organization saw efforts made to make the publication of *The Final Call* monthly, whereas previously its distribution had been irregular.[12]

The 1980s required that some changes to Elijah Muhammad's teachings were necessary and perhaps inevitable. Evidence of this surfaced in 1984, in an event that brought the Nation of Islam to the attention of the national press.

Elijah Muhammad had always questioned the logic of participating in a political system that seemed to be merely a mechanism for subjugating Blacks. In *The Message to the Blackman* he wrote:

> Certainly there is power in voting if there is justice for the so-called
> Negroes. But the crooked political machine of America can always

---

[9] Interview with Abdul Wali Muhammad, Editor, *The Final Call*, May 23, 1986.

[10] *The Final Call*, May, 1979, p. 3.

[11] Interview with Abdul Wali Muhammad, Editor, *The Final Call*, May 23, 1986.

[12] *Ibid.*

keep the once-slaves, free slaves.[13]

While the Messenger did not eliminate the possibility that American Blacks could one day meaningfully exercise their right to vote, the tone of his writing indicates he thought it highly improbable.

1984, however, saw Jesse Jackson's campaign for the leadership of the United States' Democratic Party, and Louis Farrakhan's support of his candidacy. On February 7, Farrakhan announced to the press that he would, for the first time, register to vote, [14] and three days later, he led over one thousand Blacks to a mass voter registration at Chicago's City Hall.[15] Jesse Jackson's candidacy thus marked a turning point for the Muslims. While there was no doctrinal change, accomodation of a more politically active Black population and a seemingly less race-conscious America had occurred. As C.E. Lincoln stated:

> Their position before was that there was no point in participating
> in the political process because all of the people running for office
> were white and that since all whites were alike – intrinsically evil
> – then there was no point in voting for any candidate.[16]

Jackson's campaign became a symbolic event for American Blacks. It made possible once again the dream of a more equal involvement in national politics, and a less race-conscious America. Embodying such politically important goals, it understandably became the focus of strong sentiments. Not the least of those swept up in Jackson's campaign was Minister Louis Farrakhan. Through-

---

[13]Elijah Muhammad, *The Message to the Blackman in America*, (Chicago: Muhammad's Mosque of Islam No. 2, 1965), p. 218.

[14] *The Chicago Tribune*, February 7, 1984, p. 4.

[15] *The Chicago Tribune*, February 10, 1984, III, p. 4.

[16] *Ibid.*

out the campaign, the strength of his emotional involvement was evident in his speeches.

Indeed, while he felt Jackson's chance of winning the Democratic leadership were good, Farrakhan's optimism was reflected in a toning down of his political rhetoric. In what appears retrospectively an unusually conciliatory statement, Farrakhan appeared to be moving towards de-eschatologizing the Nation's doctrine:

> The resurrection of black people is the key to a peaceful world. Caucasian people have a chance to outgrow their immature behaviour. And when we rediscover the power of God in ourselves, we see less and less of the devil in them.[17]

This optimistic comment was unique, however. Farrakhan soon returned to the piercing political remarks that had always characterized his rhetoric.

By April of 1984, the intensity of Jackson's campaign had increased, and with it, the level of tension amongst his supporters. At this point Jackson made a serious political blunder. Within earshot of Black reporter Milton Coleman, he referred to Jews as Hymies, and to New York as Hymie Town.[18] This aside was of course made public, and its revelation was a deep blow to Jackson. Incensed by the fact that Coleman would publish such remarks, Farrakhan reacted strongly, calling Coleman "a no good filthy traitor," and threatening that "One day soon we will threaten you with death."[19] Farrakhan later explained his comments as referring to a future time in which Blacks governed their own state:

> ... we will judge betrayers and traitors and treasonous behaviour

---

[17] *The Chicago Tribune*, February 26, 1984, IV,p. 5.

[18] *The Chicago Tribune*, April 4, 1984, p. 2.

[19] *Ibid.*

as all intelligent civilized nations do, and the punishment under certain circumstances is death.[20]

While comprehensible in terms of the Nation's doctrine, his comments created a public uproar and did little to help Jesse Jackson. Nevertheless, Jackson initially refused to disassociate Farrakhan from his campaign.[21]

In interviews following this incident Farrakhan continued to make remarks apparently aimed at shocking the American public. Not only did he call Zionism "a gutter religion," and deem Adolph Hitler a "wickedly great man" (for raising Germany up out of the ashes), [22] but he criticized Michael Jackson for projecting a "female-acting sissified image" that would ruin Black youth.[23]

Farrakhan's statements regarding Zionism were easy targets for the press, and left him open to charges of anti-semitism. Although he was later careful to clarify himself regarding the differences between Judaism and Zionism, he has persistently been called an "anti-semite."

The recurring anti-Zionist theme in most of Farrakhan's writing and speeches springs from two sources. First is the Jewish American's association with the Black ghetto. For many Blacks, Jews were perhaps the most commonly confronted Whites; as store owners and rent collectors they were easily resented. Their ability to transcend their social conditions, leaving behind those who had contributed to their wealth, increased Black resentment.[24] Second, and perhaps of more importance, is the Nation's tie to other Muslim communities. For them, the existence of the state of Israel must stand as a permanent barrier

---

[20]Louis Farrakhan, *Tony Brown's Journal*, Public Broadcasting System, May 23, 1985, (Transcribed from a recorded tape).

[21] *The Chicago Tribune*, April 10, 1984, p. 11.

[22] *The Chicago Tribune*, April 15, 1984, V, p. 11.

[23] *The Chicago Tribune*, April 11, 1984, p. 1.

[24]Louis Farrakhan, *Tony Brown's Journal*, Public Broadcasting System, May 23, 1985.

between Jews and Muslims. Those who support Israel are the enemy.

Although criticism of Farrakhan's remarks is often warranted, it should be noted that a great deal of his coverage in the media is biased. Exemplifying this tendency, Christopher Hitchens of *The Spectator* stated:

> It is anti-semitism that supplies the emotional energy of his entire crusade. Without it, he would have nothing to say ... Without it his whole attempt to construct a race theory ... would fall of its own weight.[25]

The Muslims' doctrine is complex; inaccurate reductionism serves only racism in another form.

Amidst the flurry of press coverage that occurred following his anti-Zionist remarks, Louis Farrakhan attended a meeting of Black Church leaders, (including the Rev. Jesse Jackson), in New Orleans.[26] Although attendance at an ecumenical meeting was new to Farrakhan, the purpose of the conference was not; the leaders hoped to convert spiritual unity into economic power.[27] The inclusive language that was later to characterize Farrakhan's eschatological warnings surfaced at this meeting. Rather than emphasizing salvation through the program of the Nation of Islam, Farrakhan stated simply, "I say the church is the last hope of black people for economic salvation."[28]

As the leadership campaign progressed, it was clear from Louis Farrakhan's statements that he had come to identify the possibility of Jackson's failure with the Fall of America. Unlike the eschatological statements made by the Honorable Elijah Muhammad, Farrakhan's warnings during this period were

---

[25]C.H. Hitchens, "The False Messiah who Hates Jews," *The Spectator*, January 25, 1986, p. 13.

[26] *The Chicago Tribune*, April 10, 1984.

[27] *Ibid.*

[28] *Ibid.*

primarily contingent on events in the political realm. As well, his appeals at this time were not just directed towards Muslims. His vision of the future involved the action of all Black Americans.[29]

As his brash political statements became more frequent, they were accompanied by more vehement apocalyptic predictions. In the April 15 edition of *The Chicago Tribune* he stated:

> The end of America is now in sight. You could save your miserable lives, but you're too filthy and wicked. You hate me for warning you. You hate me for defending another servant of Almighty God, my brother, Rev. Jesse Jackson. Before 1986 comes in, we will close out both books – the Bible and the Holy Koran – and the world will be in the throes of that which will destroy every power that is on this earth in preparation for a new gospel ... [30]

Farrakhan's connection of Jesse Jackson's campaign with the Fall of America became even clearer when, one week later, he warned that if Jackson was shut out of the Democratic leadership he would

> lead an army of black men and women to Washington D.C., and ... sit down with the president, whoever he may be, and negotiate for a separate state or territory of our own.[31]

Jesse Jackson eventually criticized Farrakhan's many remarks concerning Jews; [32] he termed Farrakhan's comments "unconscionable and reprehensible."[33]

---

[29]This openness has continued within the Nation. To this day, the Muslims are careful to stress that their faith is inclusive. Interview with Abdul Wali Muhammad, Editor, *The Final Call*, May 23, 1986.

[30] *The Chicago Tribune*, April 15, 1984, V, p. 1.

[31] *The Chicago Tribune*, April 22, 1984, III, p. 1.

[32]Louis Farrakhan, *Tony Brown's Journal*, The Public Broadcasting System, May 23, 1985.

[33] *Ibid.*

Farrakhan contended this repudiation was made under pressure from the Democratic National Committee and was based on erroneous information. [34] With respect to this, he remarked:

> The more they dumped on Farrakhan, the stronger I got, and the more support I got with the masses of Black people. That should say to the moguls and that wicked kabal that control television, "This is a different era, a different time, and that's a different kind of man." [35]

The Democratic convention was in many ways a disappointment for Minister Louis Farrakhan. Not only was Jesse Jackson unsuccessful in his bid for the leadership, but many motions put forward by him were defeated. As well, Walter Mondale's choice of running mate, Geraldine Ferraro, did not please him. He stated on *Nightwatch* that through this action "Mr. Mondale slapped Jesse Jackson and all other Blacks in the face." [36] Jackson's powerful speech was lauded by many, but Farrakhan could only note that speeches alone did not produce jobs or food for Blacks. The dream of upper-level representation in Washington had faded.[37] The entire enterprise left Farrakhan with an unpleasant taste in his mouth. He commented,

> ... if Jesse wants to run four years from now, I'm not a prophet. I don't know what I will do, but I suspect that I have had my fill with this kind of thing, and I don't think Jesse can look forward to

---

[34]Louis Farrakhan, *Tony Brown's Journal*, The Public Broadcasting System, May 23, 1985.

[35]*Ibid.*

[36]Louis Farrakhan, *Nightwatch*, Columbia Broadcasting Corporation, July 31, 1984, (Transcribed from a recorded tape).

[37]Louis Farrakhan, *Tony Brown's Journal*, Public Broadcasting System, May 23, 1985.

my support four years from now.[38]

The apocalyptic warnings that had pervaded Farrakhan's speeches during Jackson's campaign did not completely disappear after the convention. In response to questions regarding the possibility of a race war within the United States he replied:

> ... we see that the Black community is dissatisfied, impatient, angry, and the hope that they have in America is flickering and dying. Jesse Jackson represented that hope. He fired up that hope.[39]

No apocalyptic events occurred as a result of Jackson's defeat, however, and the movement was once again faced with the problem of failure of prophecy. Rather than de-eschatologizing the Nation's doctrine, Louis Farrakhan altered the content of his prophecy. His interpretation of the Fall of America became wider in scope as he came to focus more attention on the international realm and on the Nation's ties to other Muslims. The transition in Farrakhan's prophecy was thus made easier through the natural development of the Nation of Islam.

In his prophecies of the Fall, Elijah Muhammad had focused upon the internal condition of the United States. While international events and agents were often mentioned, they did not play a major role in the apocalypse. Louis Farrakhan altered this perspective. Now more completely a part of the international Muslim community, the Nation developed a more encompassing interpretation of the Fall of America. The actions of the American government towards other states were now seen as precursors to the Fall. These doctrinal changes at first appeared occasionally in speeches and articles; they were formally announced in late 1985.

---

[38] Louis Farrakhan, *Tony Brown's Journal*, Public Broadcasting System, May 23, 1985.

[39] Louis Farrakhan, *Nightwatch*, Columbia Broadcasting Corporation, July 31, 1984.

In the November 1984 edition of *The Final Call*, the transcript of Minister Farrakhan's speech to the 15th Anniversary Celebration of the Libyan Jamahiriya was published. Entitled "War is Coming," the article emphasized the relationship of international events to the eschatological prophecies of the Bible and discussed the role of Black Americans in the coming apocalypse. His comments in that article tie the doctrine of Elijah Muhammad to a more international form of Islam. He stated:

> It is not by chance that Prophet Muhammad said that the sun of Islam would rise from the west in the latter day. It is not by chance that Prophet Muhammad said that he heard the footsteps of Bilal, an Ethiopian Black man, going into paradise before himself ... And it is not by chance that brother Muammar Gathafi in his *Green Book* has said that it is the time that the Blacks shall prevail in the world.[40]

1985 saw Louis Farrakhan initiate a nationwide tour to promote POWER (People Organized and Working for Economic Rebirth), his plan for the economic development of Black Americans. Funded by a five million dollar loan from Libya,[41] the aim of POWER is to develop an economically independent Black population, as the Honourable Elijah Muhammad attempted through the Nation's business enterprises in the 1960s. Farrakhan spoke in fifteen cities during this tour[42] but did not gain major media attention until directly prior to his meeting in Los Angeles. Once again, this attention focused on the Minister's remarks regarding Jews. Jewish leaders denounced him, and

---

[40] *The Final Call*, November 1984, p. 22. See Muammar Al Qathafi, *The Green Book, Part Three, The Social Basis of the Third Universal Theory*, (Tripoli: The Public Establishment for Publishing, Date Unknown), p. 45.

[41] *The New York Times*, September 14, 1985, p. 7.

[42] *The New York Times*, October 4, 1985, B, p. 5.

leaders of the Black community, (among them, Mayor Bradley), were hesitant to voice any support for him whatsoever. In the end, Farrakhan's meeting was a success; he drew an audience of over fifteen thousand. While some undoubtedly attended merely out of curiousity, it was clear that Farrakhan's economic message had an appeal for the Black community that spread well beyond the membership of the Nation of Islam.

It was at this time that a minor furore developed over claims made by Thomas Metzger, a former leader of the California branch of the Ku Klux Klan.[43] Metzger announced that not only had he contributed money to Minister Farrakhan, but that the two had held a number of meetings together.[44] This publicity increased criticism of Farrakhan's racial policies, for the Ku Klux Klan and the Nation of Islam appeared mirror images of one another. Abdul Akbar Muhammad, one of Farrakhan's spokesmen, eventually denied that any meetings between the men had taken place.[45] The issue of Metzger's donation was dismissed by the Nation as unimportant.

The negative publicity that arose from this incident undoubtedly contributed to the great controversy that arose regarding Farrakhan's appearance in New York, the final city on his tour. The event was to take place on October 7, (Elijah Muhammad's birthday). In New York, Mayor Koch denounced him,[46] as did Governor Mario Cuomo,[47] while the Jewish Defence League held a Death to Farrakhan march.[48] Controversy over this meeting almost eclipsed that of the Jackson/Coleman affair.

---

[43] *The New York Times*, October 3, 1985, p. 19.

[44] *Ibid.*

[45] *The New York Times*, October 4, 1985, B, p. 1.

[46] *The New York Times*, October 9, 1985, II, p. 6.

[47] *The Final Call*, December, 1985, p. 4.

[48] *The New York Times*, October 7, 1985, II, p. 4.

The Nation came to interpret the New York meeting as a version of Judgement Day. Indeed, *The Final Call* tied the New York speech to UFO sightings, and thus implicitly to the Nation's interpretation of Ezekiel's Wheel and the coming of the apocalypse:

> 60 unidentified aircraft, traveling in groups of four to six, and traveling at about 288 mph were spotted by several official sources in Tuscon, Arizona on October 7 (the morning of Minister Farrakhan's Madison Square Garden lecture).[49]

Articles in the paper refer to the New York occasion as *Al-Ghashiyah*, the Overwhelming Event. In the Qur'an these terms refer to Judgement Day.

> In the name of Allah, the Beneficent, the Merciful.
> Has there come to thee the news of the Overwhelming Event?
> Faces on that day will be downcast,
> Labouring, toiling,
> Entering burning Fire, ...
> Faces on that day will be happy,
> Glad for their striving,
> In a lofty Garden, ...
> But whoever turns back and disbelieves,
> Allah will chastise him with the greatest chastisement.
> Surely to Us is their return.
> Then it is for Us to call them to account. [50]

Although at first perplexing, the apparently hastily conceived tie of the New York gathering to Judgement Day is logical. It served two important functions

---

[49] *The Final Call*, December, 1985, p. 3.

[50] *Ibid.,*

within the movement: first, it gave meaning to the controversy surrounding the meeting, and secondly, it helped prepare members for the changes Louis Farrakhan was about to formally initiate. The Nation in its present state had been judged; it was time to move on.

Farrakhan drew a capacity audience to Madison Square Garden; over twenty-five thousand people came to hear him speak,[51] and with the exception of one incident, the meeting ran smoothly. A mysterious fire began in a back room during the speeches; the Muslims hinted that this event was part of an elaborate outside attempt to assassinate Minister Farrakhan.[52]

POWER itself was affected by the controversy that surrounded this event. As a result of the many anti-semitic accusations made against Farrakhan, Johnson Products Company, commissioned to manufacture POWER's product line, pulled out of its contract with the organization. A spokesman stated the company was afraid of possible boycotts.[53]

1986 began with Farrakhan redefining his mission within the Nation of Islam and formally declaring a new direction for the Nation.[54] For Farrakhan, the overwhelming response to his POWER lecture in New York illustrated the success of Elijah Muhammad's message. Quite simply, "the time" was of great import; Minister Farrakhan had finally reaped the benefits of the Messenger's, and his own, proselytizing.[55] This achievement signalled the necessity for change in the Nation.

In an extended interview in *The Final Call*, Farrakhan delineated Paul's

---

[51] *The New York Times*, October 8, 1985, II, p. 3.

[52] *The Final Call*, December, 1985, p. 23.

[53] *The New York Times*, October 24, 1985, IV, p. 6. A detailed account of these difficulties is provided in "Would You Buy A Toothpaste from this Man?", *The Chicago Reader*, April 11, 1986, pp. 1-36.

[54] *The Final Call*, December, 1985, p. 18.

[55] *Ibid.*

New Testament teachings on Evangelists and Pastors.[56] He stated that his eight year term as an evangelist was over, and explained:

> through my evangelical preaching thousands upon thousands of people believe ... what I teach from the Honorable Elijah Muhammad. But that is not enough. I am concerned that the charisma of an evangelical preacher will be lost if the pastoring effort is not present to back up that evangelical preaching. I do not want us to be seen as a cult, following the charismatic preaching of Louis Farrakhan ...[57]

With the transformation of Minister Farrakhan's role came changes in the Nation's practice of Islam. The first was a renewed emphasis on prayer as taught in the Qur'an. The Minister explained that this practice would have been approved by Elijah Muhammad. The Messenger had not insisted upon it during his lifetime because he did not want disbelievers "to make a mockery of a perfect form of worship."[58]

In this interview, Minister Farrakhan confirmed that the Nation was about to develop closer ties to the orthodox Islamic communities of the Middle East, and again argued that such a change was envisioned by Elijah Muhammad. Evidence of this lay in four important facts: (1) that the Prophet Muhammad's life was the basis for Elijah Muhammad's life and therefore should be the basis for the lives of all Muslims, (2) that the Qur'an given to Elijah by Farad was the best book to study, (3) that if the Prophet Muhammad were still alive, he would come to America to fight for the liberation of Blacks, and (4), that before his death, Elijah Muhammad had requested a more orthodox Mosque

---

[56] *The Final Call*, December 1985, p. 18.

[57] *Ibid.*

[58] *Ibid.*

design.[59] Farrakhan stated:

> When you put all this together, you see in the words and teachings
> of the Honorable Elijah Muhammad a desire to join the Lost Found
> Members of the Nation of Islam in the east ... to enable through
> our connection, them to learn from us, and we [sic] to learn from
> them. [60]

Louis Farrakhan thus began to move the Nation of Islam closer to a more
orthodox version of the faith, while at the same time retaining much of the
original creed.

In order to develop more fully the Nation's ties to Islamic countries, Farrakhan embarked upon an extended tour of the Middle East early in 1986.
Although the Minister was able to visit a number of countries, undoubtedly
one of the highlights of his trip was the opportunity to visit Libya. That nation,
and its leader, Colonel Muammar Qathafi, had always supported the work of
the Nation of Islam. Indeed, Qathafi had spoken at an earlier Saviour's Day
Conference.

On January 7, 1986, Ronald Reagan had issued an executive order forbid-
ding Americans to visit Libya; Farrakhan defied that order and vehemently
spoke against it. In his address to the Second World Mathaba Conference in
Tripoli, Minister Farrakhan described a dream he had that indicated Ronald
Reagan was planning to destroy Libya. The President had "put himself in the
position of chief devil."[61] This religious and political vision became more fully
developed during Farrakhan's Middle Eastern tour and with the American
bombing of Libya. Gradually, the apocalypse became contingent upon aggres-

---

[59] *The Final Call*, December, 1985, p. 20.

[60] *Ibid.*

[61] *The Final Call*, May 30, 1986, p. 19.

sive actions of the American government against other nations, particularly those which are primarily Islamic.[62] Unlike the short-lived prophecies concerning his New York appearance, this vision of the Fall of America appears reasonably permanent, for it takes into account the Muslims' new religious and political perspective. America's treatment of the "oppressed within her stomach," however,[63] remains important.

On June 25, 1986, Louis Farrakhan and the Nation of Islam filed a suit in Federal District Court against President Ronald Reagan, Secretary of State George Schultz, Treasury Secretary James Baker, and Attorney General Edwin Meese.[64] Their complaint charges that Reagan's executive order was

a violation of ... rights under the First Admendment [sic] to freedom of religion, speech and the right to travel as an American citizen.[65]

On September 2, the Government filed a motion to dismiss. The case has yet to be heard.

Three days after the Nation filed its lawsuit against the Government, an official "Welcome Home" gathering was held for Farrakhan at the Chicago Hilton; at that meeting, the Minister introduced the first six products to be sold and marketed by POWER, under the label "Clean and Fresh."[66] Although a small start, compared to the Nation's monumental efforts of the 1960s, this

---

[62]Interview with Abdul Wali Muhammad, Editor, *The Final Call*, May 23, 1986.

[63]Interview with Abdul Wali Muhammad, Editor, *The Final Call*, May 23, 1986. Minister Farrakhan discusses this point in "Power, At Last, ... Forever," a speech made in Washington, D.C., July 22, 1985.

[64] *The Final Call*, Special Edition, (Vol. 5, No. 3), p. 5.

[65] *Ibid.*

[66]Telephone Interview with Abdul Wali Muhammad, Editor, *The Final Call*, September 10, 1986.

venture indicates that Farrakhan intends to attempt to make good his promises of economic development.

The apocalypse remains an important part of the Nation's doctrine. In the January 31, 1987 edition of *The Final Call*, the sighting of three UFOs by a Japanese pilot was featured. Their appearance was tied to the Muslims' interpretation of Ezekiel's Wheel:

> The size and shape of the crafts ... leaves no doubt that the so-called UFOs (Unidentified Flying Objects) sighted were the Mother Plane and two of the "baby planes" which the Honorable Elijah Muhammad taught about ... [67]

Minister Farrakhan linked this sighting to President Ronald Reagan's actions towards the Nation,[68] and to his foreign policy.[69] He warned, "BELOVED BLACK PEOPLE, FLY TO ALLAH AND SEEK REFUGE IN HIM BECAUSE THE TIME FOR THE END OF THIS WORLD IS AT HAND."[70]

At the same time, however, the Minister continued to draw the Nation closer to traditional Islam. In late 1986, he developed and distributed a program of Qur'anic study entitled "Self Improvement: The Basis for Community Development."[71] As well, he began to adopt language similar to that which Wallace Muhammad had used in 1975. In encouraging his followers to "grow vertically," he called for a "spiritual resurrection."[72]

Future directions for the Nation of Islam seem clear: the economic activities of the group will be further developed and consolidated, and in terms of

---

[67] *The Final Call*, January 31, 1987, p. 2.

[68] *Ibid.*, p. 20.

[69] *Ibid*, p. 29.

[70] *Ibid.*

[71] *The Final Call*, January 15, 1987, p. 18.

[72] *Ibid.*

doctrine, they will move closer to traditional Islam.[73] While Farrakhan has thus led the group in a direction similar to that of Wallace Muhammad and his Muslim community, he has done so while retaining Elijah Muhammad's original millenarian teachings. This doctrine has added a power and urgency to his message that is attractive to many Black Americans.

---

[73] Although this is clear from their history, Abdul Wali Muhammad also noted these points in our discussion of May 23, 1986.

Chapter 6

MILLENARIANISM AND THE NATION OF ISLAM

... it was in prison that I first heard the teachings of the Honorable Elijah Muhammad. His teachings were what turned me around ... in 1946, I was sentenced to 8-10 years in Cambridge, Massachusetts as a common thief who had never passed the eighth grade. And the next time I went back to Cambridge was in March 1961, as a guest speaker at the Harvard Law School Forum.[1]

Malcolm X

From its inception, the Nation of Islam has been influenced by its doctrine of the Fall of America. The Muslims' interpretation of the apocalypse has both motivated and guided them; its evolution marks the group's development. The theory discussed in Chapter One provides a means by which to examine the millenarianism of the Nation. From this analysis, it is possible to draw a

---

[1]Malcolm X, "Malcolm X," *The Playboy Interview*, G.B. Golson, (Ed.), (U.S.A.: Worldview Books, 1981), pp. 48-49.

conclusion regarding the meaning of the Muslims' beliefs in the context of the United States.

The Nation of Islam emerged from the simple but powerful combination of events that characterizes the development of most millenarian movements: social upheaval and disaster. The population of the United States was in a state of flux during the early 1930s, and the Great Depression intensified this trauma.

The large migration of Blacks to the North threatened a White population faced for the first time with upholding the myth of America's founding. American Blacks were beginning their search for a new identity, both as citizens of the United States, and as a visible minority. This search required a meaningful explanation for their history, as well as a means for overcoming the difficulties of the future. Two factors in particular channelled this quest in the direction of millenarianism. The first was deprivation. As was noted in Chapter One, multiple and relative deprivation are key factors in the development of millenarian beliefs. Black Americans undeniably suffered both these forms of want. Many were uneducated and illiterate and lacked the training that would permit them upward mobility. If fortunate enough to be employed, they were relegated to low-status, low-paying jobs. The ghettos thus stagnated, both economically and socially. At the same time, White society grew wealthier. The difference between the Black and White communities' standard of living was muted during the Depression, but became glaringly obvious as America began her recovery.

A second factor that fostered the development of millenarianism was the fact that most Black slaves had been encouraged, if not forced, to adopt the Christian faith. As part of their means of interpreting the world, it was bound to affect their political beliefs. The linear time line of Christianity and its divinely-ordained end provide an ideal springboard for millenarianism, for it is merely another "leap of faith" to assume one knows when, where, why, and how that end will occur.

In consideration of these factors, the development of millenarianism among Black Americans was not surprising. Indeed, it was an almost common-sense way for individuals to understand their environment. The early success of the Nation of Islam can thus be attributed more to the relevance and power of its doctrine than to factors such as charismatic leadership.

The salvation millenarians envision is usually characterized by five qualities. It is total, ultimate, collective, this-worldly, and imminent.[2] Wallace Fard and Elijah Muhammad envisioned a future in which the world would be changed completely. After a final great battle, initiated by the Mother Ship, Blacks would rise to their rightful, superior position in the world.

Although the Nation of Islam's doctrine had always been millenarian, this particular aspect of its belief system did not become fully developed until the 1960s, coinciding with the final years of Malcolm X's involvement with the group. Within the Nation today, Malcolm X is a controversial figure, but his impact upon the movement is undeniable. In his article "From Black Muslim to Bilalian," Lawrence Mamiya refers to Malcolm's death as a "watershed event" in the Nation's history;[3] this phrase is appropriate here, both as Mamiya defines it, and in terms of the Muslims' millenarianism.

In his life and death Malcolm X symbolized a fundamental paradox within the Nation's doctrine. Converted while in prison, Malcolm was undeniably a member of the Black lower class. Through his association with the movement, his life was changed completely; he rose to become one of the most important

---

[2]Yonina Talmon, "Millenarism," in *The International Encyclopedia of the Social Sciences*, Vol. 10, p. 349.

[3]Lawrence Mamiya, "From Black Muslim to Bilalian: The Evolution of a Movement," *Journal for the Scientific Study of Religion*, 1982, 21(2), p. 140.

Black leaders of his time. Although Malcolm was in many ways exceptional, success stories such as this were common within the Nation. On a large scale, a conflict was destined to occur.

The original doctrine of the Nation of Islam encouraged hard work, thrift, and a strict morality in preparation for the fall of White society; and despite their more radical political goals, the Muslims also required that members submit to the temporary authority of the American legal system. Removed from the context of millenarianism, these guidelines for behaviour were identical to those of White Anglo-Saxon Protestants. Ironically, becoming a good Muslim necessitated that one adopt the behaviour of the White majority.

As early as 1964, Michael Parenti identified this contradiction between the doctrine's end and the means necessary to achieve it. In his article "The Black Muslims: From Revolution to Institution," Parenti noted three general trends that seemed to indicate the direction of the movement's development: (1) their evolution into what was essentially a "Negro self-improvement group," (2) their development of a strong organizational framework, and (3), their apparent inclination towards a *"modus vivendi"* with American society.[4] He concluded his article by noting the world demands that

> Despite their loftiest visions, prophets become bishops, reformers become bureaucrats, and conspirators become commissars; vitality gives way to order, fire turns to form, and blood is replaced with wine.[5]

While Parenti's predictions were somewhat premature, in retrospect, their accuracy is noteworthy.

---

[4]Michael Parenti, "The Black Muslims: From Revolution to Institution," *Social Research*, 1964, pp. 182-83.

[5]*Ibid.*, p. 194.

Although the Nation of Islam was originally comprised of members of the Black lower class, a basic change in the membership's socio-economic status gradually occurred. Through their religious beliefs, long-time members improved their standard of living and drew new, middle-class friends to the movement.[6] Mamiya discusses a number of cases that illustrate this dialectic of doctrine and economics within the Nation of Islam. For example:

> Imam Sabir Alaji and his wife taught in a Muslim school in the Bronx for a number of years. Their desire was to start their own Muslim school in the mid-Hudson ... they were recently able to buy a large house and renovate it for their school. When asked for his opinion of a class shift in the movement, Alaji replied, "But I'm not rich, I'm poor." However by all standards of socio-economic status, this young Imam ... had become middle class.[7]

Some aspects of the Nation's creed were simply incomprehensible to newer members. Mamiya cites the example of a Nashville college student who felt that copying Elijah's commitment letter by hand was ridiculous. She questioned, "Why don't they just Xerox it?"[8] Through its success, the Nation's doctrine had put itself in jeopardy of becoming irrelevant.

This transition in membership demanded a moderate theology, and it could not help but affect the way in which the group faced the problem of Elijah Muhammad's failed prophecy. A middle-class individual has sufficient standing in society and enough personal collateral to enjoy the present world. Having attained some degree of security, a "new world" might appear just as much

---

[6]Also, as discussed above, Malcolm X had been particularly successful in converting middle-class individuals as early as the 1950s.

[7]Lawrence Mamiya, "From Black Muslim to Bilalian," p. 147.

[8]*Ibid.*

a threat as a bounteous promise. The practical success of the Messenger's doctrine in this way helped ease the Nation's adjustment to the failure of Elijah Muhammad's prophecy, and ensure its continued existence.

The assassination of Malcolm X was also a "watershed event" in that it marked the beginning of the period that was to see the Fall of America. It occurred as the Muslims were beginning to expect the millennium, and was interpreted as a significant event in that context. His death was one of the final evils of the old world.[9]

The reasons for Elijah Muhammad's choice of the years 1965-1966 for the apocalypse are unclear, but it is likely that he was moved by the general social upheaval of the United States at that time. In *The Message to the Blackman in America*, he specifically mentioned the decline of the American dollar and changing weather patterns as important signs of the times.[10] While the Muslims looked unfavourably upon the Civil Rights movement, the disruption it created probably also contributed to the havoc Elijah Muhammad saw.

Because the period Elijah prophesied for the apocalypse was so lengthy, it is difficult to assess at what point its "failure" was perceived by his followers. As discussed above, *Muhammad Speaks* carried articles referring to the Fall of America throughout 1965 and 1966, but these articles varied greatly in their interpretation of the apocalypse: some referred to it as currently occurring,[11] some pushed it further into the future,[12] and others hinted that it had already partially occurred.[13] Despite these divergent perspectives, the continued emphasis on the Fall of America in *Muhammad Speaks* indicates that the belief

---

[9]*Muhammad Speaks*, July 31, 1964, p. 13.

[10]Elijah Muhammad, *The Message to the Blackman in America*, pp. 273-76.

[11]See for example *Muhammad Speaks*, July 30, 1965, p. 1.

[12]See for example *Muhammad Speaks*, Feb. 12, 1965, p. 3.

[13]See, for example *Muhammad Speaks*, Jan. 7, 1966, pp. 1-2.

was not discarded. As Carroll emphasized in *When Prophecy Failed*, religious millenarianism involves the will of a divine being; faith is the substance of things hoped for. Some Muslims may have expected the Fall to occur in early 1965, but postponing it to 1966 posed no problem for them.

The Muslims' immediate response to the "failure" of Elijah Muhammad's prophecy was silence; during 1967 and early 1968, references to the Fall of America in *Muhammad Speaks* were rare. Little evidence exists to suggest that the Muslims adopted behaviour typical of disillusioned millenarians, for example, increased proselytizing. The period of relative silence that followed its "failure" appears to have been a time of reassessment.

In the Nation of Islam's terms, the political and moral health of the United States had undergone no clear improvement during the 1960s. Although advances had been made in civil rights, the general condition of Black Americans had improved little. As well, the morality of the United States government seemed, if anything, to have declined: its involvement in Vietnam evidenced that fact. The Muslims had little reason to abandon their belief that America was doomed. It is therefore not surprising that in 1968 the prophecy once again featured prominently in *Muhammad Speaks*.

As will be recalled from Chapter Three, Elijah Muhammad's prophecies of the period were less urgent and specific than those of the early 1960s. Although they had not changed significantly in terms of their content, much of the early vigour behind them seemed to have disappeared; they lacked a sense of immediacy. The resurfacing of the prophecy might have been due in part to pragmatic reasons. At the time his prophecy re-emerged, Elijah Muhammad faced two major difficulties: apparent disunity within the group, and the need for a Black hospital on the south side of Chicago. A millenarian prophecy is an ideal means to foster unity within a group. Politically and economically it made sense for Elijah Muhammad to reintroduce the Fall as an important facet of the Muslims' doctrine. As C.E. Lincoln writes in *The Black Muslims in America*, however, it is unwise to consider the group in only these terms. The Nation of Islam was also a religious community. Indeed, it is the religious nature of the Nation that most clearly illuminates its response to the failure of Elijah Muhammad's 1965 prophecy and explains its rejuvenation in 1968.

Although in many ways the Muslims' problem was similar to that of the group studied by Festinger in *When Prophecy Fails*, their responses differed substantially. A brief examination of that study helps to explain the Muslims' behaviour in 1968. Festinger concluded that cognitive dissonance caused by the failure of prophecy would move individuals to attempt its reduction, chiefly through increased proselytizing.[14] (The pain of dissonance would be eliminated by altering the environment.) These conclusions form a cornerstone of much social science research; Festinger's case study has a clinical precision rare in such investigations, and this "scientific" aura contributes to its popularity. The inapplicability of its conclusions in the case of the Nation of Islam is therefore significant. An examination of the conditions the psychologists set for their hypothesis provides part of the explanation.

The first condition Festinger set, that the millenarian belief must be held with conviction, was true of the Nation of Islam, as was the second, a strong commitment to the belief. The Muslims were convinced of White America's imminent Fall; their commitment was evidenced by the large personal investment made by members, and the financial investment made by the Nation as a whole. A third condition, the presence of social support following the disconfirmation, was also undeniably met by the Nation of Islam. Temple communities were nothing if not tightly knit. Their cohesiveness was fostered by such factors as dietary regulations, dress and behaviour codes, and mandatory meetings.

---

[14]Leon Festinger; Henry Riecken; Stanley Schachter; *When Prophecy Fails*, (New York: Harper Torchbooks, 1966), p. 28.

All of these set the Muslims apart from other Blacks.

Two important conditions Festinger set for his hypothesis were not unqualifiedly true for the Muslims. Although the Fall of America had originally been interpreted by the Nation as a distinct event, making possible a thorough disconfirmation, the term itself was sufficiently vague to admit many interpretations. Indeed, when the millennium failed to occur, such a "reinterpretation" was one of the Muslims' first responses. The Fall of America came to refer to all events of the 1965-1966 period that evidenced the evils of the United States.[15] This altered definition of the Fall of America also made impossible a complete disconfirmation of the prophecy.

Although the Nation of Islam thus adhered closely to the conditions set by Festinger it differed significantly in terms of the nature of its millennial prophecy. The Muslims' choice of reinterpretation over proselytizing is illustrative of this fact.

In his book *When Prophecy Failed*, Robert Carroll examines Festinger's cognitive dissonance research in terms of religious groups. The difficulties he finds in this application help to explain the behaviour of the Muslims. As was noted in Chapter One, Carroll correctly stresses the fact that in religious groups, prophecy is the gift of a divine being. A god's perfect nature makes error impossible; the failure of any prophecy is therefore the result of a change in His will or lies with His mortal followers. These alternatives were more acceptable to the Nation of Islam than increased proselytizing. The Fall of America was just as much a religious as a political event.

It is difficult to assess the nature of the Muslims' millenarianism between 1969 and 1975. Although the Fall of America remained a prominent feature of the group's doctrine, there was no pattern to its interpretation. Early in

---

[15] *Muhammad Speaks*, January 7, 1966, pp. 5-6.

1969, Minister Louis Farrakhan appeared to be initiating a de-eschatologizing of the prophecy,[16] but by 1970, Elijah Muhammad was once again warning of the judgments Allah was serving upon North America.[17] These statements by the Messenger did not mark the beginning of a trend towards a more vehement belief, however, for in 1971, he spoke of the millennium in purely metaphorical terms.[18]

Events within the Nation during this time illuminate somewhat these erratic changes in the Muslims' interpretation of the Fall. As will be recalled from Chapter Three, the early 1970s were probably the most violent years in the Nation's history. Numerous murders occurred, and evidence indicated that a serious power struggle within the Nation's bureaucracy was taking place. Millenarian beliefs could be inspired from this disruption and/or used to inspire unity within the group.

A less convincing reason for these divergent interpretations of the Fall concerns the health of Elijah Muhammad. The Messenger had been ill for a number of years, and this, compounded by the fact that he was by the 1970s an elderly man, has led some to speculate upon his clarity of thought. Although this could serve as a convenient catch-all solution for the cryptic puzzle of this period, it is not a sufficient explanation. The editors of *Muhammad Speaks* and the Nation's bureaucracy could, to a large degree, control the dissemination of information to members. It is unlikely that they would allow circulation of unacceptable material. As well, there appeared to be no disruption caused to the membership by the rapid changes in Elijah Muhammad's interpretation of the Fall of America; the Muslims accepted these rapid fluctuations in doctrine.

In *When Prophecy Failed*, Robert Carroll outlines a number of criticisms

---

[16] *The New York Times*, January 13, 1969, p. 44.

[17] *Muhammad Speaks*, January 9, 1970, p. 16.

[18] *Muhammad Speaks*, February 19, 1971, p. 16.

that can be made of cognitive dissonance theory, and it is the most fundamental of these that is relevant here. Festinger's theory is based upon the premise that conflicting "cognitive elements" will yield a dissonance so painful that adherents must attempt its reduction. Carroll points out that although this assumption is logical, as an hypothesis it is unproven,

> [it] may be true but it can easily ignore the fact that most people
> live with conflicting cognitive elements and do so without attempt-
> ing to resolve any dissonance experienced.[19]

In terms of the Nation of Islam, this point is well-taken. Between 1969 and 1975, the Muslims clearly suffered cognitive dissonance. They did not, however, attempt to reduce it.

Carroll adds that such dissonance could be interpreted as functional. He suggests that people can learn from tension and conflict. When this utility outweighs the negative effects of dissonance, then dissonance-arousing information will be preferred, but "where dissonance is stronger than utility ... dissonance-reducing behaviour will be manifested."[20] For millenarians, the learning that takes place as a result of "dissonance equilibration" would seem most likely to aid them in their adaptation to reality. The Muslims' oscillation between beliefs forced them to reflect upon the Fall of America in the context of improved race relations in the United States and pressure from the international Islamic community. The many interpretations of the prophecy that emerged can in this light be seen as the product of a group undergoing adjustment, rather than of a group in turmoil. The final resolution of this question did not occur until 1975.

---

[19]R. Carroll, *When Prophecy Failed*, (London: SCM Press, 1979), p. 104.

[20]*Ibid.*

Although there were indications in the last years of Elijah Muhammad's life that the Messenger had begun to de-eschatologize the Muslims' doctrine, this process did not begin in earnest until after his death. Wallace Muhammad took advantage of the large gap his father left to make rapid changes within the Nation's belief system. As noted in Chapter Four, the doctrine of the Second Resurrection represented his first attempt at introducing a degree of moderation into the Muslims' teachings. Like his father, Wallace used the Book of Revelation to interpret the history of Black Americans. In his eyes, however, the "Second Resurrection" of the Nation was the culmination of its earthly mission; Ezekiel's Wheel now symbolized the divinely revealed community of Muslims. Wallace's reinterpretation of the Nation's eschatology was similar to St. Augustine's reinterpretation of the millennialism of Christianity. Cohn summarizes the latter's de-eschatologizing as demanding that

> ... the Book of Revelation was to be understood as a spiritual
> allegory; as for the Millennium, that had begun with the birth of
> Christianity and was fully realized in the Church.[21]

Just as the Church became the representative of the City of God, so did the Muslim community become the representation of the Black millennium.

Most of the later alterations Wallace Muhammad made to the doctrine of the Nation of Islam followed from this basic reinterpretation of the role and meaning of the community. Despite the many changes that had occurred both inside and outside of the Nation, this process of de-eschatologizing still required a fundamental change in members' cosmology. With respect to this, the most difficult changes to accept were no doubt Wallace's instruction that both Wallace Farad and Elijah Muhammad were mere mortals, and his new

---

[21]Norman Cohn, *The Pursuit of the Millennium*, Rev. Ed., (New York: Oxford University Press, 1961), p. 29.

understanding of evil.

The majority of Muslims accepted these ideas, enabling the Nation of Islam to evolve into what is today simply the American Muslim community. A distinct segment of the Nation of Islam's membership, however, could not adjust to what was, in essence, a new explanation of the world. This group found a vocal spokesman in the person of Minister Louis Farrakhan.

As was discussed in Chapter Five, in 1978 Louis Farrakhan returned to the original millenarian teachings of Elijah Muhammad. In his article "Revitalization Movements," Anthony Wallace discusses such rejuvenations, interpreting them as attempts to deal with a hostile culture. In the case of the renewed Nation of Islam, this hypothesis seems appropriate. The world Louis Farrakhan saw around him could not support the ideas promoted by Wallace Muhammad.[22]

Elijah Muhammad's millenarian doctrine continued to hold a great deal of appeal for many Black Americans. Its success was perhaps fostered by President Ronald Reagan's cutbacks in social services. For the first years of the revitalized Nation's existence, Farrakhan preached the Messenger's original apocalyptic vision; it is unclear whether he specified a date for the Fall of America. As his organization developed, however, so too did Farrakhan's interpretation of the Fall. By 1987, it had undergone three distinct changes, none of which were prompted by the failure of a millennial expectation.

Farrakhan's participation in Jesse Jackson's campaign for the leadership of the United States Democratic Party prompted his first alteration to the

---

[22]Both the Muslim community and the "Nation of Islam" insist that Louis Farrakhan did not draw large numbers of Wallace's followers with him when he left the group. Rather, Farrakhan for the most part attracted individuals new to the teachings of Elijah Muhammad. This fact seems to support Lawrence Mamiya's contention that the two groups had separate constituencies. The Blacks Louis Farrakhan drew had a different perspective on existence and faced a different set of problems than their middle class brothers.

prophecy. As was noted in Chapter Five, Minister Farrakhan came to identify the possibility of Jackson's failure with the Fall.[23] Thus as the Nation became directly involved in the political realm, the millennium became contingent upon political events. Jesse Jackson was not successful in his bid for the Democratic leadership, and Farrakhan subsequently reinterpreted his prophecy.

In 1985 the Nation once again became directly involved in the economic development of Black America through POWER (People Organized and Working for Economic Rebirth). To initiate this project, Farrakhan toured the United States, speaking to Black audiences. The furor he created culminated in New York City. The Muslims tied Farrakhan's New York speech to the apocalypse, referring to it as *Al-Ghashiyah*, the Overwhelming Event, and tying it to a number of UFO sightings. Although this interpretation appeared hastily conceived, it served two purposes. It gave meaning to the controversy that surrounded Farrakhan at that time, but more importantly, it symbolized the judgment of the Nation as it stood in 1985. This reinterpretation, however, was not a de-eschatologizing of the Fall of America. Farrakhan's interpretation of the New York event as "the Judgment" enabled him to move the Nation into another stage of development, and it cleared the way for yet another millenarian interpretation of the prophecy.

As discussed above, in 1986 Minister Farrakhan moved the Nation closer to a more traditional form of Islam. He announced that no longer would he be a mere evangelist, and initiated programs of study and prayer within the Nation. As well, his followers for the first time observed Ramadan. (Farrakhan stressed that these changes had been requested by Elijah Muhammad.)[24] To strengthen the ties between the international Islamic community and the Na-

---

[23] *The Chicago Tribune*, April 15, 1984, V, p. 1.

[24] *The Final Call*, December 1985, p. 20.

tion, the Minister embarked upon a tour of the Middle East. While he was there, international political events conspired to shape the Nation's new conception of the Fall of America.

The Nation of Islam had always maintained a pro-Arab, anti-Israeli perspective on events in the Middle East. President Ronald Reagan's aggressive behaviour towards Libya displeased them greatly. Indeed, Farrakhan tied America's foreign policy to the apocalypse. Again, the prophecy was reinterpreted to reflect the group's changed interpretation of itself. As the Muslims became more fully a part of the larger Islamic community, their millennial expectations likewise developed.

These four interpretations of Elijah Muhammad's prophecy reflect the development of the Nation of Islam. Despite the relatively rapid changes in meaning that occurred, the prophecy always retained its fundamental apocalyptic tone; it was not de-eschatologized or transformed into a mere tool of rhetoric. For the Nation of Islam, a final battle between the forces of good and evil, Black and White, remains inevitable. While Farrakhan's followers have moved closer to traditional Islam, their identity as Black Americans remains an important influence on their faith.

The Muslims' millenarian vision of the Fall of America has thus always played an important role in the organization's doctrine, and indirectly, in its historical development. Perhaps the most eloquent symbol in the Nation's cosmology, it focuses clearly upon one possible answer to the questions all Black Americans must ask. The theoretical analysis discussed above illustrates how that answer has affected the community of the Nation of Islam. It leaves, however, one important problem still to be addressed. Is the Muslims' millenarianism a social pathology or a mechanism enabling their development?

As was noted in Chapter One, a division exists within scholarly literature regarding the meaning of millenarian movements. Norman Cohn interprets them as inevitably pneumopathological, while other authors, such as Peter Worsley, emphasize their role in the development of societies. Neither of these polarized perspectives, however, can fully account for the nature of millenarian movements. While the gnosticism inherent in millenarianism cannot be denied, not all millenarian doctrines are totalitarian. A variety of factors must be considered in making a final judgment regarding any millenarian group. Yonina Talmon writes:

> The outcome of any millenarian movement depends on the histor-
> ical circumstances, on the type of society, and on the nature of
> the group in which it occurs. Of crucial importance are the degree
> of differentiation of the society, the characteristics of the religious
> and political spheres, the position of the millenarian group in the
> changing balance of power, and the group's chances to promote its
> goals through political action.[25]

During its fifty-six year history, the doctrine of the Nation of Islam has changed considerably. Any attempt to determine the nature of the group's impact, however, must consider the most salient features of their original beliefs.

Two negative features of the Muslims' original doctrine are particularly noteworthy: their racism and their withdrawal from society. The millenarian conception of the "Chosen People" was, in the Nation's case, taken to the extreme: Whites were considered intrinsically evil, and Blacks the incarnation of perfect good. This belief may have been no more than a reflection of the suffering of Black Americans, but it was still racist, and racism is a feature that has marked the most dangerous of millenarian movements (for example, National Socialism). While the Muslims' beliefs drew attention to the racial

---

[25]Yonina Talmon, "Millenarism," p. 360

tension within the United States, they no doubt reinforced the racism of many American Whites.[26]

The Muslims' withdrawal from society must also be interpreted as a negative result of their millenarianism. Initially, members of the Nation were discouraged from participating in the American political system, and from having extensive contact with White society. While this distancing helped develop their sense of self-reliance and community, it also to some extent damaged the organization and the larger political entity in which it existed. In essence, the Nation's separation made it a closed society. Although conflict within the group was rare, the outbreaks of violence that did occur were intense. The Muslims' isolation perhaps contributed to this problem. No outside influence was available to temper hostility between factions.

The Nation's withdrawal also damaged the American political community. Liberal democratic regimes require the participation of many voices to be successful. By removing itself from the political realm, the Nation denied its members a place in political life and denied the American state the opportunity to hear them. If all factions withdrew and became silent, the liberal democratic system would ultimately fail.

It was through this social isolation, however, that the Muslims became more fully a part of American society. The Nation's preparations for the Fall of America were constructive; Elijah Muhammad's call to "do for self" saw his followers improve their economic and social status, and their new religious beliefs gave the Muslims a sense of identity and community. When the millennium failed to occur, the movement was therefore not destabilized. Wallace Muhammad was able to de-eschatologize completely the Nation's doctrine; his organization is today a healthy religious community.

---

[26] It is also possible that the Nation of Islam's doctrine unintentionally aided the Civil Rights movement. The Muslims no doubt made groups such as CORE and SNCC appear moderate.

A judgment regarding Louis Farrakhan's Nation of Islam is not as easily made. The "new" Nation retained Elijah Muhammad's millenarian teachings, and in doing so also kept many of its most controversial features. Rather than moving towards the totalitarianism of Norman Cohn's vision, however, Farrakhan's organization appears to be evolving into a more orthodox religious group. Having also adopted Elijah Muhammad's doctrine of self help, it is likely that Farrakhan's followers will begin to feel more certain of their place in American political life.

The millenarianism of the Nation of Islam can, with some qualifications, be interpreted as a constructive mechanism through which American Blacks could begin to overcome the oppression they suffered. The benefits it has provided have outnumbered and been more permanent than its detrimental effects. As was noted at the beginning of this thesis, a fundamental problem facing Black Americans is their historical loss of identity and community. The Nation of Islam helped its members to resolve that difficulty.

Bibliography

ARTICLES

Anonymous. "Achievements of Elijah Muhammad." *Christian Century.* 92:301-302. March 26, 1962.

_____ "A Bitter Crusade." *Maclean's.* p. 19. Jan. 20, 1986.

_____ "Black Capitalism Muslim Style." *Fortune.* 81:44. 1970.

_____ "Black Muslim Hope: Cassius Clay." *Sports Illustrated.* 20:8. March 16, 1964.

_____ "Black Muslim Rift: Recalling the Past." *Christianity Today.* 22:42. April 21, 1978.

_____ "Black Muslims: Why Do They Look Toward Mecca?" *Senior Scholastic.* 105:11. April 21, 1978.

_____ "Black Power, Foul and Fragrant." *The Economist.* pp. 25-26. Oct. 18, 1985.

_____ "Black Wasps." *Trans-Action.* 74:52. Dec. 8, 1969.

_____ "Case History of Harry X." *Newsweek.* 76:48. July 27, 1970.

_____ "Cattle Poisoners." *Newsweek.* 75:24. March 30, 1970.

_____ "Conversion of the Black Muslims." *Time.* 109:59. March 14, 1977.

_____ "Divided Islam." *Economist.* 262:43. March 19, 1977.

_____ "Enter Muhammad." *National Review.* 14:519-521. July 2, 1963.

_____ "Farrakhan Fulminations." *Time.* 124:16. July 2, 1984.

_____ "Go Ahead Apostle." *Newsweek.* 57:58-59. March 13, 1961.

_____ "Hanafi Sect." *Christianity Today.* 21:48-49. April 1, 1977.

_____ "Holy War." *Newsweek.* 81:41. Feb. 5, 1973.

_____ "I Like the World Black." *Newsweek.* 61:27-28. May 6, 1963.

_____ "Integration." *U.S. News and World Report.* p. 20. March 16, 1964.

_____ "Malcolm X." *Nation.* 200:239. March 8, 1965.

_____. "Messenger Departs." *The Economist.* 254:69. March 8, 1975.

_____ "Messenger Passes." *Time.* 105:83. March 10, 1975.

_____ "Muhammad Speaks." *Newsweek.* 79:23. Jan. 31, 1972.

_____ "Muslim Influence Great." *Science Newsletter.* 88:165. Sept. 11, 1965.

_____ "Muslim Message." *Newsweek.* 60:26-27. Aug. 27, 1962.

_____ "Muslim Rivalry." *Christianity Today.* 17:53-54. Feb. 16, 1973.

_____ "Muslim Way." *Newsweek.* 80:106. September 1972.

_____ "Muslims Farm." *Newsweek.* 74:52. Dec. 8, 1969.

_____ "Muslims in Alabama." *Time.* 95:12. Feb. 12, 1970.

_____ "Muslims vs. Muslims." *Newsweek.* 81:61. Feb. 3, 1973.

_____ "Nation of Islam Mourns." *Ebony.* 30:74-81. May 1975.

_____ "New Move by the Black Muslims." *U.S. News and World Report.* 54:14. March 11, 1963.

_____ "Now it's Negroes vs. Negroes in America's Racial Violence." *U.S. News and World Report.* 58:6. March 8, 1965.

_____ "Original Black Capitalists." *Time.* 93:21. March 7, 1969.

_____ "Religious Split at Back of Killings." *U.S. News and World Report.* 74:83. Feb. 5, 1973.

_____ "Results Behind Bars." *Time.* March 31, 1961.

_____ "Thirty-Eight Hours: Trial by Terror." *Time.* 109:14-20. March 21, 1977.

_____ "The Totalitarian, Anti-Semitic Party." *National Review.* 36:12. July 27, 1984.

_____ "Vendetta By Rivals Feared." *Senior Scholastic.* 86:21. March 11, 1965.

_____ "Washington Seige." *The Economist.* 262:43. March 12, 1977.

_____ "Whatever Happened to the Black Muslims?" *U.S. News and World Report.* 69: 83-84. Sept. 21, 1970.

_____ "Why Black Muslims are Focussing on the Nation's Capital." *U.S. News and World Report.* 54:24. May 27, 1963.

_____ "White Muslims." *Time.* 105:52. June 30, 1975.

Ansari, Zafar Ishaq. "Aspects of Black Muslim Theology." *Studia Islamica.* 53:137-176. 1981.

Arnold, E. "Message From Leader." *Esquire.* 59:97-101.

Bakewell, J.D.X. "Brotherhood Crusade." *Black Scholar.* 7:22-25. March 1975.

Balk, A. and Haley, A. "Black Merchants of Hate." *Saturday Evening Post.* 236:68-75. Jan. 26, 1963.

Berger, M. "Black Muslims." *Horizon.* 6:48-65. Winter 1964.

Beynon, E.D. "The Voodoo Cult Among Negro Migrants in Detroit." *American Journal of Sociology,* 43:894-907. May 1938.

Black, Edwin. "Would You Buy A Toothpaste From This Man?" *Chicago Reader.* pp. 1-36. April 11, 1986.

Boggs, X.J. "Beyond Malcolm X." *Monthly Review.* 29:30-48. Dec. 1977.

Bunn, C.G. "Prayers and Profits." *Black Enterprise.* 14:28. Dec. 1983.

Capouya, E. "Brief Return to Mecca." *Saturday Review.* 48:42. Nov. 20, 1965.

Clayton, Dawn. "The Daughters of Malcolm X and Martin Luther King Team Up." *People.* Sept. 5, 1983.

Cooper, C.L. "Aftermath: The Angriest Negroes Revisited." *Esquire.* 55:164-66. June 1961.

Copage, E. "Farrakhan on the Road." *Life.* 7:51-54. August 1984.

Cowley, S.C. and Weston, M. "Yesterday's Message." *Newsweek.* 85:71. June 30, 1975.

Crawford, M. "Ominous Malcolm X Exits." *Life.* 56:40. March 20, 1964.

Cripe, C.A. "Religious Freedom in Prisons." *Federal Probation.* March 1977.

Farrakhan, L. "Farrakhan on the Crisis in Black Leadership." *Essence.* 15:87. June 1984.

Flanagan, Thomas. "The Mission of Louis Riel." *Alberta History.* Vol. 23. 1975: 1-12.

Goldman, Peter. "Malcolm X: An Unfinished Story." *New York Times Magazine.* pp. 28-30. Aug. 19, 1979.

Goldman, Peter. "Who Killed Malcolm X?" *New York Times Magazine.* 93:39. May 7, 1979.

Goldman, P. and Watson, M. "Founding Father." *Newsweek.* 85:21. March 10, 1975.

Haley, A. "Malcolm X." in *The Playboy Interview.* Golson, G.B., (Ed.) U.S.A.: Worldview Books, 1981. pp. 37-53.

Hitchens, C. "The False Messiah Who Hates Jews." *The Spectator.* pp. 12-13. January 25, 1986.

Isaacs, H.R. "Integration and the Negro Mood." *Commentary.* 34:487-92. Dec. 1. 1962.

Jones, K.M. "A Model Marine Takes a Stand." *Essence.* 15:60. November 1984.

Jones, O. Jr. "Black Muslim Movement and the American Constitutional System." *The Journal of Black Studies.* 13:417-437. June 1983.

Khan, Robert A. "The Political Ideology of Malcolm X." *The Journal of Religious Thought.* 38:16-33. Fall/Winter, 1981-82.

Kidd, J.L. "Yes Sir, Mr. Ali." *Christian Century.* 85:1383-85. Oct. 30, 1985.

Kitzinger, Shiela. "Protest and Mysticism: The Rastafari Cult of Jamaica." *The Journal for the Scientific Study of Religion.* 8:240-63. 1969.

Klausler, A.P. "Muslim Rally in Chicago." 78:372. March 22, 1961.

Knoll, E. "Jesse Jackson's Claque." *Progressive.* 48:4. August 1984.

Krosney, H. "America's Black Supremacists." *Nation.* 192:390-92. May 6, 1961.

Lincoln, C.E. "Extremist Attitudes in the Black Muslim Movement." *Journal of Social Issues.* 19:75-85. Spring 1963.

Lincoln, C.E. "The Meaning of Malcolm X." *Christian Century.* 82:431-33. April 7, 1965.

Lincoln, C.E. and Mamiya, L. "Black Militant and Separatist Movements." in *Encyclopedia of Religion in America.* C.E. Lippy and P.W. Williams, (Eds.). (Charles Scribner's Sons: 1986).

Linn, E. and Bainette, A. (Eds.). "Black Muslims are a Fraud." *Saturday Evening Post.* 238:23-29. Feb. 27., 1965.

Maesen, W. A. "Watchtower Influences on Black Muslim Eschatology." *Journal for the Scientific Study of Religion.* 9:321-25. Winter 1970.

Mahrer, J. "Negro Racists." *Nation.* 196:278. April 6, 1963.

Mamiya, L.H. "From Black Muslim to Bilalian: The Evolution of a Movement." *The Journal for the Scientific Study of Religion.* 21:138-52. June 1982.

Massaquoi, H.J. "Elijah Muhammad." *Ebony.* 25:78-80. August 1970.

Mathews, T. "Seizing Hostages." *Newsweek.* 89:16-20. March 21, 1977.

Maule, T. and Russell, B. (Eds.). "I'm Not Worried About Ali." *Sports Illustrated.* 26:18-21. June 19, 1967.

Meer, Fatima. "American Impressions." *Reality.* pp. 11-15. July 1973.

Muhammad, A. "Civil War in Islamic America." *Nation.* 224:721-24. June 11, 1977.

Muhammad, W.D. "Stepping Down and Moving On." *Christianity Today.* 23:45. Oct. 6, 1978.

Muwakkil, Salim. "Louis Farrakhan and the Rhetoric of Racial Division." *In These Times.* 9:40.

North, D. "Democrat's Dilemma." *Maclean's*. 97:18-19. July 9, 1984.

O'Gara, J. "After Malcolm X." *Commonweal*. 82:8. March 26, 1965.

O'Gara, J. "Muhammad Speaks." *Commonweal*. 78:130. April 26, 1963.

O'Gara, J. "Muslims, Black and White." *Commonweal*. 77:428. Jan. 18, 1963.

Olsen, J. "Learning Elijah's Advanced Lesson in Hate." *Sports Illustrated*. 24:36-38. May 2, 1966.

Parenti, Michael. "The Black Muslims: From Revolution to Institution." *Social Research*. 31:174-94. 1964.

Parks, G. "White Devils' Day is Almost Over." *Life*. 54:22-23. May 31, 1963.

Payne, R. "Why 4,000,000,000 Follow Muhammad." *New York Times Magazine*. p. 18. Aug. 14, 1963.

Plimpton, X.G. "Miami Notebook: Malcolm X and Cassius Clay." *Harper's*. 228:54-61. June 1964.

Southwick, A.B. "James Baldwin's Jeremiad." *Christian Century*. 82:362-64. March 24, 1965.

Southwick, A.B. "Malcolm X, Charismatic Demagogue." *Christian Century*. 80:740-41. June 5, 1963.

Starr, M. "Jackson Disavows Farrakhan." *Newsweek*. 104:16-17. July 9, 1984.

Talmon, Yonina. "Millenarism." in *International Encyclopedia of the Social Sciences*. D.L. Sills, (Ed.).

Tinney, J.S. "Bilalian Muslim." *Christianity Today*. 20:51-52. March 12, 1976.

Tinney, J.S. "Billing the Baptists." *Christianity Today*. 19:49-50. Oct. 25, 1974.

Tinney, J.S "Black Muslims: Moving Into Mainstream." *Christianity Today*. 17:44-45. Aug. 10, 1973.

Tinney, J.S. "Kansas City Church Building Dispute." *Christianity Today*. 17:54. May 25, 1973.

Tinney, J.S. "State of the Nation." *Christianity Today.* 20:42-43. March 26, 1976.

Whitehurst, J.E. "Mainstreaming of the Black Muslims." *Christian Century.* 97:225-29. Feb. 27, 1980.

Wieseltier, L. "Naked Lunch." *New Republic.* 191:43. Aug. 27, 1984.

Williams, D.A. and Sciolino, E. "Rebirth of the Nation." *Newsweek.* p. 33. March 15, 1976.

Wilmore, G.S. Jr. "My Face is Black." *Christian Century.* 82:82. Jan. 20, 1965.

Woodward, K.L. "Tough Rules of Brotherhood." *Newsweek.* 104:80-81. July 16, 1984.

Woodward, K.L. and Davis, N. "Second Resurrection." *Newsweek.* 90:67. Aug. 22, 1977.

Worthy, M. "The Angriest Negroes." *Esquire.* 55:102-5. June 1961.

Zygmunt, J.F. "Prophetic Failure and Chiliastic Identity: The Case of the Jehovah's Witnesses." *American Journal of Sociology.* 75: 926-48.

BIBLIOGRAPHIES

Brinkerhoff, M. *Religion and Charisma.* (Unpublished).

Hexham, I. *A Bibliographical Guide to Cults, Sects, and New Religious Movements.* Winnipeg: Institute for Social and Economic Research. No Date.

Johnson, Timothy V. *Malcolm X, A Comprehensive Annotated Bibliography.* New York: Garland Publishing Inc., 1986.

Townsend, J.B. *Selected Religion Bibliography: Special Emphasis On Revitalization Studies.* (Unpublished). 1973.

BOOKS

Abdul-Rauf, Muhammad. *Bilal Ibn Rabah, A Leading Companion of the Prophet Muhammad.* Takoma Park: American Trust Publications, 1977.

Adas, Michael. *Prophets of Rebellion – Millenarian Protest Movements Against the Colonial Order.* Chapel Hill: University of North Carolina Press, 1979.

Akbar, Na'im. *Chains and Images of Psychological Slavery.* Jersey City: New Mind Productions, 1984.

Akbar, Na'im. *The Community of Self.* Rev. Ed. Tallahassee: Mind Productions, 1985.

Baldwin, James. *The Fire Next Time.* New York: Dell Publishing Co., 1962.

Barkun, Michael. *Crucible of the Millennium, The Burned-Over District of New York in the 1840s.* Syracuse: Syracuse University Press, 1986.

Barkun, Michael. *Disaster and the Millennium.* New Haven: Yale University Press, 1974.

Barkun, Michael. (Ed.). *Millenarian Change: Movements of Total Transformation, American Behavioral Scientist, Special Edition.* 16:2. Nov./Dec. 1972.

Benz, Ernst. *Evolution and Christian Hope: Man's Concept of the Future from the Early Fathers to Teilhard de Chardin.* Trans. H.G. Frank. Garden City: Anchor Books, 1968.

Breitman, George. *Malcolm X on Afro-American History.* Expanded Edition. New York: Pathfinder Press, 1970.

Breitman, George. (Ed.) *Malcolm X Speaks, Selected Speeches and Statements.* New York: Grove Press, Inc., 1965.

Breitman, G.; Porter, H.; and Smith, B. *The Assassination of Malcolm X.* New York: Pathfinder Press, 1976.

Carroll, Robert P. *When Prophecy Failed, Reactions and Responses to Failure in the Old Testament Prophetic Traditions.* London: SCM Press Ltd., 1979.

Chambers, B. and Moon, R. Eds. *Right On! An Anthology of Black Literature.* New York: Mentor Books, 1970.

Clarke, John H. (Ed.). *Malcolm X, The Man and His Times.* Toronto: The Macmillan Co., 1969.

Cohn, Norman. *The Pursuit of the Millennium.* Revised Edition. New York: Oxford University Press, 1970.

Curtis, Richard. *The Life of Malcolm X.* Philadelphia: McRae Smith Co., 1971.

Douglas, Mary. *Natural Symbols*. London: The Cresset Press, 1970.

Draper, Theodore. *The Rediscovery of Black Nationalism*. New York: The Viking Press, 1969.

Essien-Udom, E.U. *Black Nationalism*. Chicago: University of Chicago Press, 1961.

Fauset, Arthur H. *Black Gods of the Metropolis, Negro Religious Cults of the Urban North*. Philadelphia: University of Pennsylvania Press, 1944.

Festinger, Leon; Riecken, Henry W.; and Schochter, Stanley. *When Prophecy Fails*. New York: Harper and Row Publishers, 1976.

Goldman, Peter. *The Death and Life of Malcolm X*. New York: Harper and Row Publishers, 1973.

Halsell, Grace. *Prophecy and Politics, Militant Evangelists on the Road to Nuclear War*. Westport: Lawrence Hill and Co., 1986.

Harrison, J.F.C. *The Second Coming, Popular Millenarianism 1780-1850*. London: Routledge and Kegan Paul, 1979.

Hill, Christopher. *The World Turned Upside Down*. Harmondsworth: Penguin Books, 1975.

Hobsbawm, E.J. *Primitive Rebels, Studies in Archaic Forms of Social Movements in the 19th and 20th Centuries*. New York: W.W. Norton and Co. Inc., 1959.

Lanternari, Vittorio. *The Religions of the Oppressed – A Study of Modern Messianic Cults*. New York: A. Knopff, Inc., 1963.

Lincoln, C.E. *The Black Muslims in America*. Revised Edition. Boston: Beacon Press, 1973.

Lincoln, C.E. *My Face is Black*. Boston: Beacon Press, 1964.

Lomax, Louis. *When the Word is Given*. New York: World Publishing Co., 1963.

Marsh, Clifton E. *From Black Muslims to Muslims: The Transition from Separatism to Islam, 1930-1980*. Metuchen: The Scarecrow Press, 1984.

McGinn, Bernard. *Visions of the End, Apocalyptic Traditions in the Middle Ages*. New York: Columbia University Press, 1979.

Moorhead, J. *American Apocalypse*. New Haven: Yale University Press, 1978.

Muhammad, Elijah. *Message to the Blackman in America*. Chicago: Muhammad Mosque of Islam No. 2, 1965.

Muhammad, Jabril. *Farrakhan: The Traveler*. Phoenix: PHNX SN & CO., Inc., 1985.

Muhammad, Jabril. *A Special Spokesman*. Phoenix: PHNX SN & CO., Inc., 1984.

Muhammad, W.D. *As the Light Shineth From the East*. Chicago: WDM Publishing Co., 1980.

Muhammad, W.D. *Challenges that Face Man Today*. Chicago: WDM Publishing Co., 1985.

Muhammad, W.D. *Imam W. Deen Muhammad Speaks from Harlem, N.Y.* Chicago: W.D. Muhammad Publications, 1984.

Muhammad, W.D. *Prayer and Al-Islam*. Chicago: Muhammad Islamic Foundation, 1982.

Muhammad, W.D. *Religion on the Line*. Chicago: W.D. Muhammad Publications, 1983.

Nu'man, Muhammad A. *New World Leadership*. Jersey City: New Mind Productions, 1984.

Nu'man, Muhammad A. *What Every American Should Know About Islam and the Muslims*. Jersey City: New Mind Productions, 1985.

Oliver, John A. *Eldridge Cleaver Reborn*. Plainfield: Logos International, 1977.

Penton, M.J. *Apocalypse Delayed – The Story of Jehovah's Witnesses*. Toronto: University of Toronto Press, 1985.

Peters, Ted. *Futures – Human and Divine*. Atlanta: John Knox Press 1978.

Quathafi, M. *The Green Book*. Tripoli: Public Establishment for Publishing, No Date.

Rhodes, J.M. *The Hitler Movement – A Modern Millenarian Revolution*. Stanford: Hoover Institute Press, 1980.

Rose, Peter I. *Old Memories, New Moods*. New York: Atherton Press, 1970.

Sahib, Hatim. *The Nation of Islam.* M.A. Thesis, University of Chicago. 1951.

Smart, Ninian. *The Religious Experience of Mankind.* 2nd Ed. Glasgow: William Collins & Sons Co. Ltd., 1969.

Smith, Jane I. and Haddad, Yvonne Y. *The Islamic Understanding of Death and Resurrection.* Albany: State University of New York Press, 1981.

Sundkler, B.G.M. *Bantu Prophets in South Africa.* 2nd Ed. London: Oxford University Press, 1961.

Tabb, William K. *The Political Economy of the Black Ghetto.* New York: W.W. Norton & Co. Inc., 1970.

Thrupp, Sylvia. Ed. *Millennial Dreams in Action – Studies in Revolutionary Religious Movements.* New York: Schocken Books, 1970.

Voegelin, E. *The New Science of Politics.* Chicago: University of Chicago Press, 1952.

Wallis, Roy. Ed. *Millennialism and Charisma.* Northern Ireland: Queen's University Press, 1982.

Weber, Timothy. *Living in the Shadow of the Second Coming.* New York: Oxford University Press, 1979.

Williams, A. Ed. *Prophecy and Millenarianism, Essays in Honour of Marjorie Reeves.* Burnt Hill: Longman House, 1980.

Wilson, Bryan R. *Magic and the Millennium.* New York: Harper and Row, 1973.

Wolfenstein, E.V. *The Victims of Democracy.* Berkeley: University of California Press, 1981.

Wolseley, Roland E. *The Black Press, U.S.A.* Ames: The Iowa State University Press, 1971.

Worsley, Peter. *The Trumpet Shall Sound - A Study of 'Cargo' Cults in Melanesia.* London: Granada Publishing, 1957.

X, Malcolm with Haley, Alex. *The Autobiography of Malcolm X.* New York: Ballantine Books, 1973.

INTERVIEWS

Muhammad, Abdul Wali. Editor, *The Final Call.* Chicago, Illinois. Interview, May 23, 1986.

Muhammad, Abdul Wali. Editor, *The Final Call.* Chicago, Illinois. Telephone Interview, September 10, 1986.

Muhammad, Bilal. Imam, Toronto, Ontario. Interview, January 3, 1986.

Muhammad, Nuri. Associate Editor, *The Muslim Journal*, Chicago, Illinois. Interview, May 19, 1986.

Muhammad, Nuri. Associate Editor, *The Muslim Journal*, Chicago, Illinois. Telephone Interview, March 12, 1987.

NEWSPAPERS

The American Muslim Journal. 1980-1985.

The Bilalian News. 1975-1980.

The Chicago Tribune. 1972-1986.

Community Voice. II:4. June 1982.

The Final Call. 1979-1987.

Muhammad Speaks. 1961- 1975.

The Muslim Journal. 1985-1987.

The New York Times. 1960-1986.

Progressions. May-July, October, November 1985.

RECORDED SPEECHES

Akbar, Na'im. *Power from Black History.* Jersey City: New Mind Productions, No Date.

Akbar, Na'im. *The Psychological Effects of Racial Images.* Jersey City: New Mind Productions, No Date.

Akbar, Na'im. *Restoration of African Consciousness.* Jersey City: New Mind Productions, No Date.

Farrakhan, Louis. *Power, At Last ... Forever!* Los Angeles, California. Sept. 14, 1985. Chicago: POWER.

Farrakhan, Louis. *Power, At Last ... Forever!* Washington, D.C. July 22, 1985. Chicago: POWER.

X, Malcolm. *The Ballot or the Bullet.* Jersey City: New Mind Productions, No Date.

X, Malcolm. *The Black Man's History.* Jersey City: New Mind Productions, No Date.

X, Malcolm. *Malcolm X Speaks to the People of Harlem.* Jersey City: New Mind Productions, No Date.

X, Malcolm. *Message to the Grass Roots.* Jersey City: New Mind Productions, No Date.

X, Malcolm. *Prospects for Freedom – 1965.* Jersey City: New Mind Productions, No Date.

TELEVISION PROGRAMS

CBS. *Nightwatch.* July 31, 1984.

PBS. *Tony Brown's Journal.* May 23, 1985.

Appendix A

WHAT THE MUSLIMS WANT

By Elijah Muhammad

1. We want freedom. We want a full and complete freedom.

2. We want justice. Equal justice under the law. We want justice applied equally to all, regardless of creed or class or color.

3. We want equality of opportunity. We want equal membership in society with the best in civilized society.

4. We want our people in America, whose parents or grandparents were descendants from slaves, to be allowed to establish a separate territory of their own ...

5. We want freedom for all Believers of Islam now held in federal prisons. We want freedom for all black men and women now under death sentence in innumerable prisons in the North as well as the South. We want every black man and woman to have the freedom to accept or reject being separated from the slavemaster's children and establish a land of their own ...

6. We want an immediate end to the police brutality and mob attacks against the so-called Negro throughout the United States.

7. As long as we are not allowed to establish a state or territory of our own, we demand not only equal justice under the laws of the United States, but equal employment opportunities – NOW ...

8. We want the government of the United States to exempt our people from ALL taxation as long as we are deprived of equal justice under the laws of the land.

9. We want equal education – but separate schools up to 16 for boys and 18 for girls on the condition that the girls will be sent to women's colleges and universities. We want all black children educated, taught without hindrance or supression.

10. We believe that intermarriage or race mixing should be prohibited. We want the religion of Islam taught without hindrance or supression.

This statement is taken from *The Message to the Blackman in America*, pp. 161-62; it was published in every issue of *Muhammad Speaks* until 1975. Currently it may be found in every edition of *The Final Call*.

Appendix B

THE TRUTH

The Truth as revealed by Allah, in the
Person of Master Fard Muhammad, to
Messenger Elijah Muhammad, verifies the
Truth of th Bible and Holy Qur-an.

By Elijah Muhammad

1. IT IS TRUE that we must come face to face with God in the resurrection.

2. IT IS ALSO TRUE that we must come face to face in the reality of the devil.

3. ALLAH HAS TAUGHT MUHAMMAD that the white race is the devil.

4. IT IS TRUE that the Lost-Found so-called Negroes are members of the Divine Family.

5. IT IS TRUE that the scriptures verify the truth that we must be returned again to our own.

6. IT IS TRUE that before they can be returned they must first have a knowledge of self.

7. IT IS TRUE that the Black Nation has no birth record.

8. IT IS TRUE that the white race (the devils) had its beginning 6,000 years ago and its time was limited to that period of time (6,000 years).

9. IT IS TRUE that they have lived and ruled the darker people under evil, filth, indecency and deceit. They have built a world of sport and play.

10. IT IS TRUE, according to the scripture of both the Bible and Holy Qur-an, that God would, on finding the Lost members, set those who believe into heaven. This is true, according to the great change in the lives of Muhammad and his followers.

11. IT IS TRUE that there will be a display of the power of Allah (God) against the wicked to whom the Lost-Found members are in subjection.

12. IT IS TRUE that Messenger Muhammad is now warning this government that Almighty God Allah has numbered America as being number one on His list for destruction because of the evil done to His people, the Lost-Found members of the original Divine People of the earth, with storms, rain, hail, snow, and earthquakes. These plagues of judgment are now going on over America.

13. IT IS TRUE that we are now being called by the white man's names. It is equally true that the Bible teaches us that on the resurrection we must accept the name of God, which shall live forever, if we are to see the Hereafter. This warning, Messenger Muhammad warns us, the so-called Negroes, daily.

14. IT IS TRUE, according to the religious scientists of both Christianity and Islam, as both agree that this year 1966, of the Christian calendar, and which is 1386 of the Arabic calendar, is the fateful year of America

and her people, and that the so-called Negroes should fly to Allah and follow Messenger Muhammad, for refuge from the dreadful judgments that Allah has said that He will bring, and which have already begun upon America.

This statement is published in *Muhammad Speaks*, April 1, 1966, pp. 1-2.

Index

STUDIES IN RELIGION AND SOCIETY